Recycled Childhood

Also by J.C. Pater

The Lost Boys from Longwood

RECYCLED CHILDHOOD

Foster Care: The Heroes, the Victims,
and the Abusers. True Stories.

J.C. Pater

CONTENTS

CHAPTER ONE

The Abused and the Abusers

The 20th century brought a radical change to the way we view and treat children. In his book of essays, *The History of Childhood*, an American scholar and a social thinker, Lloyd de Mause, wrote, "The history of childhood is the nightmare from which we have only recently begun to awaken."

Mause did not mean that in the past, parents did not love their children. Both historical and archeological data provide multiple examples to the contrary. For example, when Medieval parents gave their young child away to join a convent at the tender age of six, it was not because they were trying to get rid of the child. It was because in the Middle Ages, people were deeply, almost fanatically religious, and they were making a sacrifice by giving God what they considered most precious. At the same time, they were providing the child with perhaps the only opportunity to get educated and have a relatively safe future.

Similarly, history's tendency of having marriages between very young children had nothing to do with sexual abuse, which was actually more common among nobles than commoners. The purpose was to strengthen and increase the wealth and the prestige of both families. The marriage would usually not be consummated until both children were ready.

However, for centuries and perhaps millennia indulgence toward children was viewed as something much worse than harsh discipline. People quoted the Bible, saying "spare the rod, spoil the child" (Proverbs 13:24). If you were not using corporal punishment with your kids, you were considered a bad parent. All children were required to exhibit unquestionable obedience toward parents, other adult relatives, and all grownups with whom they interacted. Any sign of insubordination would be punished swiftly and violently. Giving a severe beating to a child was universally accepted and encouraged.

Children were loved but also viewed as property. Parents owned them and could do whatever they wanted with them without being judged. In many cultures, parents had the right to give away or even kill their children. By no means was it frequent, but there are historical cases of such events. Even infanticide - the killing of a newborn child - was, to some extent, acceptable, especially among the lower classes. Contraception did not exist, and for a woman, infanticide was safer than abortion. If the mother knew that her child would be starving, she might choose to kill it, and the death of a bastard child might have been preferable to a life of shame for both the mother and the newborn. Infant mortality was rampant, and according to current estimates, during the Middle Ages and the Renaissance, between thirty and fifty percent of children died before reaching the age of eighteen. People were used to losing children. With medical knowledge practically nonexistent, they were more focused on ensuring that a child would have a proper afterlife than if the child actually would have a life of its own. A baby would be baptized immediately after being born, and if it died afterward, so be it.

The children who survived the first hours and days of their lives could die in the upcoming months due to an accident, disease, or as a result of some bizarre practice. For example, in Medieval Europe, babies were routinely swaddled, or tightly wrapped in strips of linen and immobilized, unable to move any part of their body, including their arms and legs. Newborns looked like Egyptian mummies because people believed that babies were too fragile to be allowed to move.

The age of sexual maturity was usually twelve for girls and fourteen for boys, but criminal liability started at the age of ten. There are records of a ten-year-old boy sentenced to death by hanging and a thirteen-year-old girl executed by burning. Children, who were thrown to dungeons for such crimes as stealing bread, usually did not survive.

Additionally, the rapid expansion of industry resulted in an exponential increase in child labor. As recently as the 1900s, around eighteen percent of American workers were under the age of sixteen. Since labor laws did not yet exist, many children were worked to death.

And now, let's fast forward to 2020. A female art teacher in a public school in Illinois was suspended because, while walking around the classroom and checking students' work, she would sometimes put her hand on their shoulders. Somebody complained, and the school district agreed that touching a child was unacceptable, regardless of the intentions.

In another school, parents yelled at a teacher because their teenage son would not do homework, would not pay attention in class, would get an F on most tests and quizzes, and, consequently, was failing the class. Parents, however, blamed the teacher. Somewhere else, an eleven-year-old threw a tantrum and smashed his mother's cherished china set after she told him to stop playing a video game at one in the morning on a school night. A fifteen-year-old female walked into the classroom ten minutes late and talking loudly on her cell phone. When the teachers politely asked her to put away the phone and sit down, she yelled, "Shut up! Can't you see I'm on the phone?" Another fifteen-year-old female shared her sexually explicit photos on social media. When deeply concerned school administrators contacted her parents, the mom said, "Oh, leave her alone. They are young, and they have to explore!" And finally, have you ever been on a plane and had to sit next to a screaming toddler whose parents did not believe in disciplining or even redirecting their child? After a couple of hours, you might convince yourself that jumping off the plane without a parachute would be a perfectly reasonable solution.

How, on Earth, did we go from one extreme to the other? When did our children switch from being abused to becoming abusers?

Partial blame can be put on society, which has drastically re-evaluated norms of conduct concerning family relations. Nowadays, parents do not spend enough time with their children because parents are notoriously busy. Even the term "parents" has been redefined since we are now practicing serial monogamy. It is not uncommon for a child to say, "I have just spent a weekend with my dad and his third wife. I really like Robby, my dad's third wife's son from her first marriage, but I cannot stand Debbie, my father's daughter from his first marriage. Unfortunately, I cannot see Robby next weekend because I have to babysit my little half-sister from my mom's current marriage." After hearing this, any decent person from the Middle Ages would promptly perform an exorcism.

Grandparents, who in the past were often an anchor, binding the family and helping with the kids, are now absent. Have you noticed that, compared to all other mammals – or, in fact, all other animals – humans live for a long time beyond their age of procreation? It is a nice adaptation developed by our species. Since human children require an exceptionally long time before they mature, and must be taken care of until it happens, grandparents would historically perform the role of caretaker while parents were out hunting, gathering food, or performing other essential functions to ensure that the family survives. Unfortunately, that tradition has ended because today, grandma and grandpa are enjoying their golden years in Florida.

Another common feature of our advanced society is a single mom performing all duties traditionally assigned to a male and a female. Mom is working a full-time and a part-time job. She comes home exhausted to cook, clean, and do laundry. Late at night, she still has to fix a broken faucet and check the angry-sounding sump pump in the basement. When she finally goes to bed to get her five hours of sleep, the last thought that crosses her mind is, "I have finally become the man I always wanted to marry!"

That overworked mom may leave her ten-year-old daughter home alone. The girl has a running nose and a fever, and mom must make a quick trip to Walgreens to get over-the-counter cold medication. She does not want to drag the sick child with her. Another mom has her two-year-old finally asleep in his car seat after he was screaming for an hour. Mom has to pull over at the gas station to get milk and would hate to wake him, so she leaves the child alone in the car. Both moms are breaking the law, and both may face serious consequences. Both may lose their kids to Child Protective Services, at least temporarily.

Disciplining your child is now restricted, regulated, and in many cases, illegal. A Medieval peasant wife did not have more time to spend with her kids than a contemporary hard-working mother, but when her child misbehaved, she spanked him. Today, when an exhausted mom cannot handle her son, spanking is out of the question. Instead, she runs to the store to buy him something he wants and bribe him into obedience. In the process, she teaches her child to misbehave whenever he wants to get something new.

Severe child abuse and neglect did not end in some bygone era. They are still very much alive. Because children are small, weak, and trusting, they are easy targets, and this is why we have laws to protect them. If a child is starved, tortured, or sexually abused, everyone agrees that a state agency designated for this role should step in and take the child to safety.

However, there are gray areas where moral and ethical problems abound, and not so many people agree: where exactly is the end of parental rights and the beginning of child abuse? When a child is throwing a tantrum because a parent dares to say "No" to his or her unreasonable demand, do parents have the right to spank him? What is the definition of spanking? One slap at the child's bottom with a palm of a hand and within specific parameters defining the impulse-momentum relationship, and measured in Newtons?

Allowable discipline is ambiguous. A parent could face legal repercussions for spanking a child in California, but not in Texas. Or vice versa. Leaving a child home alone for an hour may be considered perfectly reasonable in one jurisdiction but not in another. So, what is the definition of neglect, and how much does it differ among states?

In 1993, soon after the release of *Home Alone 2*, David and Sharon Shoo, affluent parents who lived in a suburb of Chicago, took a lovely vacation in Mexico, leaving their four- and nine-year-old daughters home alone for Christmas. Two days after they left, a fire alarm went off in the house, and the terrified girls ran to the neighbors. The neighbors called the police, and the parents were contacted and ordered to return. They were arrested upon arriving at the airport but ended up with just a two-year probation following a misdemeanor plea deal. At the time, nobody really knew how to deal with the case because laws defining child abandonment and tying it to neglect either did not exist or were vague.

Today, we are faring better in this respect, but existing regulations are still far from perfect. Some states dictate a minimum age for leaving a kid home alone, while some have only loose recommendations. For example, in Oregon, it applies to children younger than ten, but in Maryland, the law only includes kids below the age of eight. There is also an unclear interpretation of what is considered abandoning a child. Is it leaving the kid home alone overnight? Or maybe for an hour?

Finally, there is the issue of parents' intentions. There is a significant difference between a mom who left a seven-year-old home alone and went to a bar for a drink, and a mom who did not make it home on time when her seven-year-old came from school because her supervisor demanded that she stayed at work after hours. Clearly, the supervisor could not care less about her young child or her family obligations, but is that enough to make the mother legally in the wrong?

Laws may be biased against the poor by not taking into consideration that some single mothers, trying desperately to provide for their children, may have limited options with arranging proper supervision. From time to time, the media would report horror stories about overzealous bureaucrats who placed someone's kids in a foster home to punish a mother who was just trying to make ends meet.

While this discussion continues and deserves more attention than it is currently getting, the purpose of this book is to focus on issues related to unquestionable abuse and neglect. It is about children who were truly tormented, about monster parents, about amazing or horrible foster homes, and about cases in which Child Protective Services came too late or did not do enough to save a child.

CHAPTER TWO

Protective Services

After a child is removed from a home that is deemed unsafe, responsibility for that child falls to the state. The same applies to children who become orphaned and have no living relatives willing and able to care for them. The federal government is not directly involved in the majority of these instances.

Most wards of the state, or youth in care, are placed in foster homes. Foster parents are required to ensure that a foster child will have appropriate shelter, enough food, and necessary clothing. Foster parents are also expected to provide other necessities and supervision. According to data released by the federal Department of Health and Human Services, at the end of 2017, the number of American children in foster care was close to 443,000. Unfortunately, the number of children removed from homes is on the rise, increasing by approximately six thousand compared to the previous year.

Over 100,000 children in foster care were available for adoption in 2017. However, only seven percent were babies less than one-year-old, and only eight percent were toddlers, which typically represents the two most popular and desirable age groups in terms of adoption. Forty-four percent of children in foster care were white, followed by African American children at twenty-three percent, and Hispanic children at twenty-one percent.

Although requirements vary from state to state, to become a foster parent, a person typically must be at least twenty-one-years-old. Additionally, a potential foster parent and all members of his or her household must pass a criminal background check. He or she also has to receive at least twenty-four hours of training, although some states require even more time. He or she must be financially stable. The average approval process takes three months. Single foster parents are welcome, but married couples are tacitly preferred. In recent years, there has been little progress regarding homosexual and lesbian couples. In many states, especially when foster care is supervised by private agencies, some with religious affiliations, same-sex couples are not considered for placement, although this is not spelled out in procedural guidelines. They will obtain a license but – with few notable exceptions - will never have foster kids placed with them.

A foster parent must have his house or apartment approved before a child can move in. It is not required that foster parents are wealthy or own a big house, but the residence must be safe, have a fire escape plan, clean water, and a designated place where a child can sleep and keep his or her belongings. A foster child does not have to have a separate room, but must have a bed since he or she cannot share a bed with a foster parent or sibling. People who live on private wells must have their water tested. It is also frequently required that the water heater is set up at a lower level to prevent accidental scalding.

According to data compiled by ABC News, American taxpayers spend twenty-two billion dollars per year on foster care programs, although that number includes children placed with relatives and wards of the states who live in group homes. This number amounts to approximately $50,000 per foster child per year.

On the other side of the process, children are removed from homes because they are abused or neglected by their biological parents. The scope of this phenomenon is, to say the least, shocking. Every day, four to seven children die in the United States as a result of abuse. Reports of abuse of children are made every ten minutes. Based on data released by the federal Department of Health and Human Services, Administration for Children and Families, in 2016, almost 1,750 children died in the United States from abuse, neglect, or maltreatment. Although this number is smaller than that of 2015, it is still a six percent increase since 2011. Part of the reason for this increase could be improvement in reporting, but historical data also indicates that child abuse has a direct correlation with poverty levels. Abuse is closely related to poverty, and according to the report issued by the US Census Bureau and published by Children's Defense Fund, in 2017, seventeen and a half percent of American children - almost thirteen million kids - lived in poverty. Nearly six million children – about one in twelve – lived in extreme poverty, which is defined by an annual income of $12,642 for a family of four. The number of kids living in extreme poverty was equal to the entire population of Maryland, and a little more than the population of Wisconsin. The even more disturbing fact: nearly half of those children were under the age of five.

National data also indicated that in 2017, almost 700,000 children in the United States were abused. More than seventeen percent were victims of physical abuse and eight-and-a-half percent were sexually abused. In four out of five cases, the person responsible for abusing a child was a parent or a caregiver. Almost half of the abused children were less than one-year-old, and another third were between the ages of one and three. 1,720 children died from abuse or neglect, which amounts to losing between four and seven children everyday. The United States has one of the worst records among the industrialized nations.

CHAPTER THREE

Little Victims from Illinois

In the past seven years, the Illinois Department of Children and Family Services has had ten directors or acting directors. During his campaign, the former Republican governor of Illinois, Bruce Rauner, criticized his predecessor, Pat Quinn, for not doing enough to prevent the deaths of Illinois children. One of Rauner's campaign commercials stated, "They were just children. Our most vulnerable with their whole lives ahead. Lives cut short tragically, senselessly from abuse, neglect while in the care of Pat Quinn's administration." True to his words, soon after his inauguration, Governor Rauner appointed George Sheldon as the new director of DCFS and called him the "best of the best." Sheldon announced sweeping reforms, changing a culture, and working with fidelity. DCFS introduced forty new initiatives. *Chicago Tribune* wrote about a significant overhaul within the department, and reasons to be optimistic that such changes would do some good.

One year later, George Sheldon resigned amid an ethics probe and alleged nepotism. More than anything else, however, Sheldon's career in Illinois was shattered by the case of little Semaj Crosby.

When Semaj died, she was only seventeen-months old. Before her death, Semaj lived with her mom and three siblings in a tiny house in Joliet Township, Illinois. Semaj was supposed to live there with just her mom and siblings, but at some point, DCFS received an anonymous tip that thirty people were living in the house, and that fifteen of them were children. It deserves mentioning that Semaj's mom had some cognitive limitations. Her only income was $773 per month in disability checks. She qualified for Section 8 housing assistance, which is how she got her Joliet place. For just Semaj, her mom, and her siblings, the place would probably have been sufficient, but the mom always had squatters living there. The house was described as filthy and deplorable. Trash and cockroaches were everywhere. People slept in broken beds or on the floor. Semaj's mom had no car.

In the twelve months preceding Semaj's death, DCFS conducted eleven investigations following reports of alleged child abuse going on in the house. There were twenty-three allegations of child endangerment. Only two were founded, eleven were unfounded, and ten were still pending. In March 2017, the DCFS hotline received a report of a three-year-old girl being molested in Semaj's house. The girl was taken to a hospital with swelling of her private parts, bruises, and belt buckle marks all over her little body, but it was concluded that there was no penetration. In the eyes of DCFS, everything was fine.

DCFS later explained that they do not punish people for being poor or for having dirty houses. However, the department was involved. Hours before Semaj's disappearance, a caseworker visited the home and brought bunk beds for the kids and cleaning supplies for mom. The mom promised that she would clean the place and assemble the beds.

Soon after the caseworker left, Semaj was reported missing. Local law enforcement organized a massive search that lasted thirty hours. Finally, the girl's body was found underneath a couch inside her filthy house. For some reason, nobody noticed that there was a dead child in the room. Nobody knew how or why little Semaj died, and many questions regarding her death remained unanswered. The investigation was hampered because the house burned down only hours after Semaj's funeral. Police suspected arson. The media kept asking why, after so many reports, DCFS did not do more to prevent Semaj's death.

In November of 2015, also in Illinois, two-year-old Eliana Claiborne was beaten to death by her mother, a sixteen-year-old runaway. An autopsy showed that Eliana had scars all over her body, bruises on her head, stomach, face and back, burn marks on her feet, and two fractured ribs. DCFS was involved before the tragedy, but explained that they could not prevent Eliana's death because of poor communication between the department and a private agency contracted to assist the family. Following Eliana's death, her mother was arrested, and while in jail, gave birth to another child.

When Jazmine Walker, age six-months, died in Illinois in May of 2017, her weight was only five pounds. The cause of death was starvation. Jazmine's death probably saved the lives of her two older brothers who, according to the medical report, were "showing signs of wasting." There were reports that DCFS visited the kids just eight days before Jazmine's demise. Once again, according to their report, everything was fine.

Although the death of a child is always tragic, few cases have been more disturbing than the death of a four-year-old Chicago boy, Manny Aguilar. Loyal to the trend, Child Protective Services were involved before it happened. At some point, Manny's mom, Alyssa Garcia, even lost custody of all her children, but they were later reunited. After a child protective agency decided to return the boys to their abusive mother, Manny's two older brothers texted their former foster mom to report that they were beaten, scared to death, and wanted out. The issue was resolved by taking away their cell phones. Everything was fine, and the children reporting their abuse no longer bothered the caseworkers. From time to time, a caseworker would even drop by to check on the kids. Before her visits, the mom coerced Manny and his brothers to keep quiet and behave. If they did as told, they would get water and something to eat.

Manny lived in his own feces and urine in an unheated storage room. At first, he had the company of the family dog, but the dog later died of hypothermia. During that time, Manny's twenty-seven-year-old mother lived with her seventeen-year-old boyfriend, who had a long record of twenty-two juvenile arrests.

One cold night, in February 2016, Manny was banging on the door of his icy prison, pleading for water. The mom was busy watching TV and told Manny's brothers to ignore the noise. After a while, when the storage room fell strangely quiet, one of the older brothers was sent to check on Manny and found him dead.

The mom, her boyfriend, and another friend tried to cover up Manny's death. First, they attempted to conceal Manny's identity by knocking out his teeth with a base-ball bat. They did it because they once saw a TV show about identifying a body based on dental records. To be identified based on dental records, one must have dental records, which Manny did not because he never went to a dentist. But the TV show did not cover that little detail. After knocking out Manny's teeth, the mom and her friends moved his body to the trunk of a car. In a couple of days, it started to smell, and the air freshener did not help much. Finally, they wrapped Manny's body in a blanket, put it in the basement of an abandoned house, and lit it on fire. When firefighters found the remains, Manny's body was so small that they thought it was a baby. Once again, one child's tragic death saved the lives of his siblings because, following Manny's death, DCFS took his brothers into protective custody.

The story of the Quate sisters was equally gruesome. In 2017, the skeletal remains of six-year-old Alysha Quate were found inside a storage tote filled with cat litter in an abandoned garage in Centerville, Illinois. The exact cause of death would never be established because no autopsy could be performed. After four years, the body was too decomposed.

There were reports that DCFS investigated the Quate family at least three times. One incident involved a school principal who reported that the girls' father, Jason Quate, gave one of his older daughters an open mouth kiss while dropping her off at school. At that time, the older girls were in the second and third grades. After the principal intervened, the girls were removed from school and homeschooled by their loving father.

At first, when Alysha died, her body was kept on the dining room floor, but later, it was hidden in the abandoned garage. The family escaped to Nevada. After a while, Alysha's mom, Elizabeth Quate, could no longer look at herself in the mirror, went to a shelter, and reported to local authorities that her husband was forcing her into prostitution and that he was abusing their two girls. She also told authorities about Alysha, who at that time had been dead for four years.

When Las Vegas police entered the apartment occupied by the Quates, they were met by a sight that disturbed even the most seasoned cops. Alysha's two older sisters had not been allowed to leave the apartment for at least eighteen months. They were not enrolled and did not attend school. They had scars and bruises all over their bodies, and one girl's hair was falling out in clumps. They were small, pale, and thin. According to the police reports, the girls were laying pantless on two separate mattresses and showing signs of severe abuse. They needed support just to walk to the police car. At that time, the girls were eleven and thirteen-years-old.

According to news reports, Jason Quate admitted to killing Alysha. He was also facing other charges in two states. Some of them included sexual assault on children, committing open or gross lewdness with a child, severe mental and bodily harm, sex-trafficking, accepting and receiving earnings of a prostitute, and possessing child pornography.

All of these cases had one thing in common: Illinois DCFS was involved before the child died. People reasonably questioned whether these deaths were preventable. There were newspaper reports stating that to eliminate the backlog, DCFS, or at least some DCFS offices, were engaged in dubious practices, such as rewarding employees with gift cards for closing abuse and neglect cases within a month. Investigations take time and cost money and, therefore, were not encouraged. Allegedly, other incentives for closing abuse cases included allowing employees to claim overtime rather than comp time. When investigations were concluded, and claims of abuse were unfounded, DCFS records were destroyed after only one year.

The current governor of Illinois, a Democrat named JB Pritzker, was inaugurated in 2019. He pledged seventy-five million dollars and one hundred additional new staff as part of a reform to boost the agency's monitoring power. Although Pritzker's pledges were not different from the ones made by his predecessors, to his credit, Pritzker acknowledged that there could be a problem with privatizing child care in Illinois. The governor ordered an investigation into the practice of referring eighty-percent of DCFS cases to private child care agencies without adequate oversight. Between July of 2017 and June of 2018, Illinois reported ninety-eight deaths of children in DCFS care. Eighteen were homicides, and twenty-six were undetermined. More than one-third of the dead children were under the age of three.

Governor Pritzker appointed a new acting director of DCFS, who said that he was "absolutely in the process of doing some reorganization." Then, Illinois was shaken by the death of little AJ Freund, but that story deserves its own chapter.

CHAPTER FOUR

AJ

AJ's mom was an attractive blond who did well at school, played basketball, and ran track and field. While at school, she was never in trouble. She was a talented artist, and showed enough promise to attend an invitation-only art camp for students. AJ's dad was a lawyer. In high school, he earned the title of Junior-class prom prince and was described as a "most desirable date." A son of an architect, he graduated with honors from the University of Illinois in Urbana-Champaign and later earned a law degree from John Marshall Law School in Chicago.

Two perfect parents, with a good upbringing, living in a safe suburb of Chicago – this should be a story about a happy childhood, right? Wrong. This is a story about not making assumptions, because monster parents can come in many forms. In this case, their child, not even six-years-old, was found in a shallow grave. The artist and the lawyer were indicted on sixty-one counts of murder, aggravated battery, concealing a homicide, and the list goes on. In an unprecedented move, the Illinois Department of Children and Family Services initiated a process to terminate three of its employees involved with the case. The case of little AJ, or Andrew Freund Jr., is a story about everything that is wrong with our opioid and drug-addicted society and our often-impotent Child Protective Services.

AJ's mom, JoAnn Cunningham, was a promising young artist until she got pregnant at the age of sixteen. She dropped out of school, moved in with her boyfriend and his family, and gave birth to a boy. She later earned her GED. Just before her son was born, JoAnn inherited $50,000, but that money was quickly spent on a new car and a boat. JoAnn spent ten years living with the father of her first child, although they were never married. Their relationship was described as rocky, and there were indications that JoAnn might have been physically abused. During that time, she also went through the shock of losing her brother, who committed suicide at the age of twenty-one. JoAnn's brother had cocaine and marijuana in his system.

When she was twenty-three, JoAnn left her boyfriend and moved back in with her mother, Lori Hughes. The mom was very supportive of her daughter and her five-year-old grandson. JoAnn was able to complete cosmetology school and obtained a license. She started dating again and eventually married Craig Summerkamp, a former US marine and veteran of the war in Iraq. He was the opposite of JoAnn's chaotic and abusive boyfriend.

Around that time, JoAnn started taking painkillers, and soon became addicted. Her medications were first prescribed after she complained about chronic back pain due to fibromyalgia, but when her prescriptions ran out, JoAnn started buying the meds illegally. Her regiment included Norco, Percocet, and morphine. At one point, she took between twelve and fifteen painkillers per day.

In less than three years of marriage, her husband filed for a divorce, accusing JoAnn of irrational behavior and excessive violence. She asked for financial support, but the judge denied her request, stating that there was no viable reason for JoAnn not to seek employment. JoAnn was also ordered to stop selling her ex-husband's belongings.

When JoAnn was crying in a courthouse during her divorce proceedings, she was approached by a middle-aged man. He was a lawyer, twenty-five years her senior, and his name was Andrew Thomas Freund. Freund provided JoAnn with a shoulder to cry on and offered to represent her for free. This chance meeting was the beginning of a long, dysfunctional relationship between two damaged individuals and addict, and it ended in the murder of JoAnn's child.

Freund's early years were even more promising than Cunningham's. He was a diligent and talented student, he earned a law degree, and was hired by a law firm in Crystal Lake, Illinois. Nobody knows what happened between the start of a promising career and the law firm asking him to leave due to blatant abuse of alcohol, and possibly opioids. For the next fifteen years, Freund practiced law from his house and supplemented his income by working part-time in a local grocery store. The once-promising lawyer was bagging groceries and stocking shelves.

Soon after their chance meeting in the courthouse, JoAnn moved in with Freund. Living together was the beginning of a fast-tracked downward-spiral for both of them. It was so bad that JoAnn's mom started calling the DCFS hotline with serious concerns about her grandson. She reported that her daughter was mentally unstable, abusing drugs, neglecting her child, and living in squalor. The house had no heat, running water, or a working phone; the floors were covered in dog waste, there were dirty dishes everywhere, and piles of cat-urine soaked laundry. There was no food for the child.

Eventually, in 2013, grandma Hughes was awarded permanent custody of her grandson. A few days before the court issued that decision, JoAnn gave birth to another son.

AJ Freund, the son of a once-pretty artist and a promising lawyer, came into the world on October 14, 2013, and was immediately in trouble. He was born through an emergency cesarean section, weighing only five pounds and seven ounces and, according to a detailed report of the case published by the *Chicago Tribune*, exhibited "tremors, sneezing, excessive crying, sleep disturbance, and an overreactive startle reflex." While very pregnant, mommy showed restraint, and on the day AJ was born, took only some derivative of heroin, and three medications for anxiety and pain.

Grandma Hughes came running to the hospital and warned the personnel that JoAnn was not fit to be a mother, and under no circumstances should they release the baby to her. At that point, however, nobody was releasing the baby to anyone. Due to his extensive medical needs, AJ had to stay in the hospital for a month. When he finally stabilized, he went to a foster home. His foster mother was a relative, JoAnn's cousin. She soon fell in love with the baby and expressed a sincere intention to adopt him. However, family courts and Child Protective Services typically work hand in hand to ensure the return of a child to biological parents.

In the meantime, there was mounting evidence of problems. A few days after AJ was born, a plumber called to Freund's house reported to the police that there was black mold, garbage, and animal excrements all over the place, not to mention several inches of standing water in the basement. While AJ stayed with her cousin, JoAnn went back to the hospital after a heroin overdose. The loving dad was also busy – drinking, taking opioids, and using cocaine. Child Protective Services made attempts to visit the parents and show them their new baby, but nobody was home. At least, nobody opened the door. Neither Cunningham nor Freund made any attempts to see their child, but this did not discourage the court and Child Protective Services to continue their relentless efforts to reunite AJ with his parents. The caseworker described Cunningham and Freund as "loving and appropriate."

It would be unfair to say that nothing was done to ensure AJ's safety. His parents were ordered to attend therapy, and they complied. They were subjected to frequent drug tests, which were negative, at least most of the time. Soon after, JoAnn gave birth to her third child, another boy, and was allowed to take the baby home.

The couple also took renters to supplement their meager income, which came mostly from stealing items from local stores. They faced a real possibility of losing their house due to over $25,000 in back property taxes, and to prevent it from happening, they promptly set up a GoFundMe page showing the pictures of their babies. They ignored the fact that AJ was not yet living with them and that they were not interested in seeing him after he was born.

Finally, in June 2015, AJ was reunited with his biological parents. Freund and Cunningham remained under supervision for almost a year. Freund regained his license to practice law. Everything looked good, and in April 2016, Freund and Cunningham were awarded full custody of their son, AJ, who was two-and-a-half at that time. The case was closed.

The first indications of impending disaster came in fall of the following year. The parents did not enroll AJ in school. They did not take him to a doctor for his annual checkup. They finally lost the house due to unpaid property taxes, but the tax buyer let them stay there in exchange for a $100,000 mortgage. They never made a single payment. JoAnn broke all ties with her family. She stopped returning their phone calls. On Halloween, a neighbor noticed extensive burn marks on AJ's body. JoAnn explained that he had an accident, but there was no record that he ever received treatment.

At that time, AJ's parents took another roommate, Daniel Nowicki Jr., a heroin addict who soon also became JoAnn's lover. Her behavior became more and more erratic. She was found confused and barely responsive in a car, forty miles away from her house, and was taken to a hospital. When Freund and the boys came for a visit, hospital personnel notified DCFS that AJ had "odd bruising to his face and forehead," and that the boys looked dirty and neglected. DCFS followed up and sent an investigator, Kathleen Gold. She went to the wrong house. She did not see AJ until a month later, but by that time, his bruises were gone.

On another visit to a hospital, JoAnn ended up attacking a nurse, and was charged with battery. She was spending $100 per day on drugs. This amount of money would provide her with a daily supply of ten to fifteen bags of heroin, and people noticed. The neighbor called authorities several times, asking to send someone to check on the kids since the house was unkept, did not have working utilities, and was a scene of frequent loud fights. In the meantime, the romance between Cunningham and Nowicki blossomed. By the end of 2018, JoAnne was pregnant with his child.

The Crystal Lake Police Department did everything they could to address the issues in AJ's residence. They took temporary protective custody of the boys, photographed the interior of the house, and documented AJ's injuries. They called the DCFS hotline, which sent another investigator, Carlos Acosta, to the home. AJ was sent to a doctor again, but the physician could not establish the cause of AJ's bruising, although she was startled when the little boy said, "Maybe someone hit me with a belt. Maybe mommy didn't mean to hurt me." She recommended further investigation, but she was ignored.

The following day, the DCFS investigator visited the house and reported that everything looked good and that the place was not in the squalid condition as described by the police. There was no follow-up about AJ's injuries. In January 2019, Acosta closed the case and deemed the hotline allegations as unfounded.

In early 2019 another grandmother entered the scene. Nowicki's mother was unable to check on JoAnn and called 911. She expressed grave concerns, especially since two small kids were living in the house. Again, nothing was done. Much later, a video from this time surfaced. It shows AJ lying on a bare mattress in a crib. He is naked except for bandages around his wrists and hips. He has two black eyes and bruises on his neck and upper chest. Supposedly, he was punished by his mother for urinating in his bed.

In April 2019, Freund called 911 and reported that his son, AJ, was missing. What followed was a massive search with an army of law enforcement and volunteers. Freund and JoAnne paraded in front of the TV cameras tearfully pleading, "AJ, please come home. We love you very much."

Six days later, AJ's body was found wrapped in plastic and buried in a shallow grave in unincorporated Woodstock, about seven miles from AJ's home. An autopsy and investigation revealed that the boy went through torturous punishments and was forced to stay in a cold shower for a prolonged period of time. He was then sent to bed wet and naked. At some point during the night, his parents found him dead. They kept the body in a tote and stored it in a basement, but after three days, Freund threw the corpse of his five-year-old son in the back of his truck, and buried it in an empty lot near Woodstock. Then, he called 911 and reported the child missing.

Following her arrest, Cunningham gave birth to her fourth child, a baby girl who was placed in a foster home. A paternity test confirmed that her biological father was Nowicki, who died of a suspected drug overdose only a few months later. AJ's little brother was also sent to a foster home. He was quoted saying that he was afraid of two things: the darkness and his mother, because "Mommy is a monster."

The grandma, Lori Hughes, blamed herself for not saving AJ. Her oldest grandson, the one she did save, is now in college and doing great. But fighting for him devoured all of Lori's money – she had to pay thousands of dollars in legal fees – and there was only so much she could afford. In the end, Child Protective Services failed to protect her grandson.

In October 2019, Illinois Department of Children and Family Services made an unprecedented announcement. They moved to terminate Carlos Acosta, Kathleen Gold, and their supervisor, Andrew Polovin.

In early December 2019, JoAnn Cunningham pleaded guilty to the murder of her son. She faces twenty to sixty years in prison.

In the first days of 2020, the inspector general of the Illinois DCFS issued a report stating that in the previous fiscal year, 123 children died within a year of becoming involved with the state's Child Protective Services.

CHAPTER FIVE

Foster Wish List

Decisions related to foster care are made by politicians, agencies providing services, and advocates who represent biological parents. Foster parents are usually excluded from these discussions. Those who take broken and abused children under their roofs, who provide not only care but healing, and who typically know children in foster care better than others, either have no voice, or their voice has no impact. The author of this publication reached out to a social media group representing foster parents and asked them to share their opinions about what can be done to improve the system.

While foster parents are sometimes viewed as leeches interested only in the financial aspect of providing care to abused or neglected children, not a single person invited to share their opinions asked for more money. Whoever has fostered, or is currently fostering a child, knows that it is never about money, and that the stipends provided by the state only cover the bare minimum. If you are genuinely invested in fostering, you probably spend more than you get.

The most common response on foster parents' wish lists was putting the best interests of a foster child first and making it a priority. When a woman is abused by her husband – or vice versa – she typically enjoys full protection from the legal system. She can obtain a restraining order. It is relatively easy for her to get a divorce. Nobody of a sound mind would require or expect her to go back to her abuser. Yet, for some reason, we have different standards for abused and neglected kids. Instead of prioritizing their safety and well-being, the system prioritizes reunification with the biological family.

Consequently, many foster children end up exactly where they started. They continue being neglected and abused, sustain severe physical and psychological trauma, and sometimes die. It should be unacceptable. A felony child abuse conviction should result in the automatic and swift termination of all parental rights. Even when a case does not result in a felony conviction, biological parents who abuse or neglect their child should follow a three-strikes rule. If a child protective agency has to intervene three times to save a child, that child should be permanently removed from the home and placed for adoption.

There were many claims that a woman who repeatedly abuses and neglects her children should be sterilized or somehow prevented from getting pregnant again. They claimed that she should not be permitted to give birth to kids who would inevitably be taken in by the foster care system.. Although perfectly logical, this approach would probably meet an immediate constitutional challenge.

Children are not property and should not be treated as such. The psychological damage caused to a child who frequently changes hands and wanders between biological parents and foster homes is immeasurable. For the same reason, a child should not be used as a carrot at the end of a stick. It is common practice for a caregiver, usually a biological mother, to be forced to start a rehab. She is generally told that if she does not comply, she is going to lose her children. Yet, when she doesn't comply, rarely does something happen. She is once again told that if she does not go to rehab, her kids will be removed. And once again, nothing happens. Eventually, she learns that no matter what she does, her kids will remain with her even if they are neglected or abused.

Additionally, the system should be more attuned to the needs of at-risk families and intervene before the circumstances are out of control, and kids must be removed. For the same reason, there should be extended supervision and support after a foster child is reunited with biological parents. The family should be closely monitored and receive assistance for at least three years following the reunification. Wishful thinking that this time everything will be fine is dangerous and foolish.

Foster parents should participate in decisions regarding a foster child, especially after that child has spent a significant amount of time in their care. Instead of being treated like babysitters, foster parents should have an equal voice at the table. They know the child better than others, and they have a proven record of acting in the best interest of a child. If a foster child is older, he or she should also participate in decisions regarding his or her fate.

Caseworkers should establish better communication with foster parents and listen to what they have to say. For example, when a foster parent recommends more counseling or less psychotropic meds for a foster child, the agency should give it serious consideration.

Foster parents who agree to take high-risk and violent kids should receive additional protection and support. When there is counseling provided to the foster parent and a foster child, it should include all members of a household. Foster siblings are frequently the ones most affected by violent outbursts. They should be taught how to recognize the signs to prevent such outbursts from happening, and how to deal with it when they do happen.

Finally, and this issue was brought up by most foster parents, cases should not be allowed to drift out into infinity. There should be firm deadlines and specific timelines. It has been recognized as a serious problem not just by foster parents but also by the powers that be. According to national data, on average, foster children remain in state care for nearly two years, while six percent languished in care for five years or more. That being said, some states are doing a better job than others. The ones at the bottom of the list are District of Columbia, Illinois, Connecticut, and New York. Kids who become permanent beneficiaries of the system often end up in residential facilities. According to some foster parents, these facilities should be shut down, since they are breeding grounds for crime, violence, and the sexual exploitation of minors.

Foster parents are hopeful that somebody will listen to their suggestions; that CASA, Guardians ad Litem, and politicians will pay attention and take notes. If they do, maybe the future AJs of the world can be saved.

CHAPTER SIX

Mike

Mike was first sexually abused when he was just three-years-old. Mike's father forced him and his five-year-old brother to do unspeakable things to each other. Sometimes Mike's father participated, but usually, he only filmed and took pictures. There is a black market for this type of filth, and through it, Mike's father generated a nice little income. Whenever the boys refused or did not perform to dad's satisfaction, they were beaten, burned with cigarettes, and denied food. With Mike, sexual abuse lasted for over four years.

Eventually, the father went to prison for unrelated crimes, and the mother relinquished custody of Mike and his brother. She was heavily addicted to meth and in no shape to care for the kids. Mike became a ward of the state.

Mike could have been a poster boy for a cute Irish-American kid. He had curly reddish hair, dimples, and an arresting smile. Finding a foster home for a white kid like him was easy. But at the age of seven, Mike rarely smiled, and he did not adapt well to his new life in foster care. Already a veteran of sexual, physical, and mental abuse, he exhibited extreme and sometimes self-destructive behaviors. On two occasions, Mike injured his caregivers with a knife. In one foster home, he deliberately set his bed on fire. Running away was the norm.

During the next six years, Mike went through an impressive number of over ten foster homes. He was hospitalized multiple times and diagnosed with a whole slew of disabilities and disorders. Mike had BD, ED, ADHD, PTSD, OCD, ODD, and a few other things with or without acronyms. On top of that, Mike, who as a young child was also underfed, hoarded his food. His foster parents frequently found spoiled milk, rotting fruit or putrid snacks hidden in the most unusual places. Mike received all kinds of therapy, but nothing worked.

Despite his inner demons, Mike became a fantastic athlete. He was a tall, strong boy and his schoolmates thought twice before starting a fight with Mike. He tried and excelled in many sports, and coaches loved him.

By the end of the seventh grade, Mike was placed in yet another foster home. His new foster parents were Anna and Lester. They lived in a single-family home with their biological son and with Trixie, a huge German shepherd dog.

Before Mike, Anna never had foster kids in her house, and Trixie was one of the reasons. Like all German shepherds, Trixie was fervently devoted to her family, yet equally skeptical of the rest of the human race. Always ready to protect Anna and her men, Trixie made sure that all other people kept an appropriate distance. If they came too close, Trixie would produce a deep growl and expose her impressive teeth. It was more than enough to keep strangers at bay. Trixie was also immensely intelligent, she acted as if she could read minds, and she definitely understood English. However, she did not bother to engage in conversation. If you were brave enough to come closer and look into Trixie's eyes, you would suspect that she possessed all the secret knowledge of the universe.

When Anna and her husband brought Mike home for the first time, they explained to Trixie that he was now family and, therefore, should not be eaten. Trixie understood and showed incredible restraint by not growling, however - just in case - exposed some of her teeth. After that, she tolerated Mike and eventually accepted him into the pack.

Anna was determined to change Mike's life. In this troubled and profoundly disturbed boy, Anna saw something exceptional and worth saving. By the end his first day in her house, Anna discovered that Mike's demons came to haunt him at night. Nights were also the time when Mike's father abused him. Nights set the stage for fear, anguish, and pain. Mike dreaded darkness; his bedroom had to be brightly lit with intense ceiling light, a nightstand lamp, and a fat rope of LED lights that Mike carried with him from one foster home to another like it was his most prized possession. The radio also had to be on.

In the morning, after the first night in their house, Anna discovered that Mike wet his bed. He also wet his bed the following night and the night after that. At night, this athletic and robust teenager, this fearless lacrosse and football player, relived his torment. Mike would wail, scream, and sob through his sleep. He was suffering from what is called night terrors, and part of it was wetting his bed.

Anna changed Mike's sheets every day, but she wanted the bedwetting to stop. Mike was in continuous therapy, and he took a cocktail of antianxiety medications that probably could have put an elephant to sleep, yet nothing seemed to work. Eventually, Anna decided to try a different approach. She explained the situation to Trixie and asked her to sleep in Mike's room.

At first, Trixie was not thrilled about the plan. She was not a therapy dog, and she was never trained to deal with people with disabilities. However, Trixie understood the gravity of the task in hand and agreed to leave her usual spot by Anna's bed.

Mike loved having Trixie in his room. When Anna quietly checked on them late at night, Mike was sleeping on the floor with his hands around Trixie's muscular neck and with his face resting on her thick coat. Trixie gently raised her head, looked at Anna, and her eyes said, "I got it covered. You may go to bed."

Mike did not wet himself that night or the next. He kept sleeping on the floor, night after night, cuddling with the huge dog. Then, he moved back to his bed with Trixie by his side. His bedwetting stopped. Finally, a few weeks later, Trixie decided to return to her old spot in Anna's and Lester's bedroom. She gave Anna that all-knowing look, which said, "My job here is done."

Mike never wet his bed again.

CHAPTER SEVEN

Foster to Famous

In recent decades, there were extraordinary individuals who managed to go from being in foster care to becoming famous. They started as children without parents, or children who received assistance from Child Protective Services. Yet, they were able to achieve fame and success.

Cher, the famous American singer and actress, had a father who was an alcoholic gambler that was rarely home. Eventually, her parents divorced. Her mom always had problems with getting a steady job and establishing long-lasting relationships. As Cher and her mother moved around the country for her mom's brief acting and singing gigs, they lived in undeniable poverty. Cher's mother was married eight times. At some point, she left Cher in an orphanage for several weeks.

Malcolm X was one of eight children of an activist Baptist minister father and a homemaker mother. The family got multiple death threats from white suprem-acists. When Malcolm was only four, their house in Michigan was burned to the ground. Two years later, his father was killed. Eventually, his mom had a nervous breakdown and was committed to a mental hospital. Malcolm and his siblings were split among orphanages and foster homes.

When his parents separated, ten-years-old Alonzo Mourning, the ex-NBA player, could not decide whether he wanted to live with his mom or dad. He ended up in the foster home of a retired schoolteacher and her husband. Over time, the couple provided foster care to almost fifty kids. When Alonzo stayed in their house, nine other children lived there.

Steve Jobs was born to an unwed mother at a time when having a child out of wedlock was not socially acceptable. His mom also put him up for adoption, and he landed in the home of a machinist who did not even graduate from high school. Steve had a turbulent child-hood, and his adoptive mother had to bribe him with money and candy to persuade him to do well at school.

Marilyn Monroe, born Norma Jean, was seven-years-old when her mother was diagnosed with paranoid schizophrenia and placed in a mental hospital. Norma/Marilyn spent the next nine years in an orphanage and in a series of foster homes. To avoid moving from one place to another, she decided to marry at the age of sixteen. Years later, Marilyn Monroe said, "No one ever told me I was pretty when I was a little girl. All little girls should be told they're pretty, even if they aren't."

Ben Nighthorse Campbell, the first Native American elected to the United States Senate in over sixty years, also had a tragic childhood. His mother was a Portuguese immigrant, and his dad was a Northern Cheyenne Indian. Ben's father grew up in a time when being a Native American was considered shameful. Like many others, he found solace in alcohol. Ben's mother was diagnosed with tuberculosis.

Consequently, Ben and his sisters spent a large part of their childhood in group homes. Even when, from time to time, they were allowed to stay home, they could not get close to their mom because TB is highly contagious. While reminiscing on his past, Senator Nighthorse Campbell said, "Little kids always hug their mothers. I could never do that."

When Eddie Murphy was five, his father died, and his mother went to a hospital. Eddie and his older brother were placed in a foster home for a year.

Many people look at Willie Nelson as a quintessential American. He traces his genealogy to the American Revolution, in which his ancestor, John Nelson, served as a major. A country music legend and a relentless fighter for the often-forgotten American farmers, Willie was abandoned by his mom soon after he was born. His father left not long after.

John Lennon, another music icon, was born in the midst of World War Two. The very first sounds he heard were the air raids by Luftwaffe dropping bombs on his hometown, Liverpool, in England. John's father was away at sea and did not see his son until John was eighteen-months-old. When he finally returned home, John's mom filed for a divorce, and John did not take it well. At the age of five-and-a-half, he was expelled from Kindergarten. John shared a bedroom with his mom and her boyfriend, which prompted child services to step in. He was removed from the home and placed with a relative.

Ice-T, or Tracy Morrow, became an orphan when his young parents died in a tragic car accident. The boy was sent to live with relatives thousands of miles away from his home. Never truly wanted and viewed only as a burden, Ice-T grew up in a rough neighborhood in South Central Los Angeles. He joined a local gang and later explained, "I first found the word *love* in a gang; I learned to love in a gang, not in the family atmosphere."

Former foster children are among celebrities, politicians, successful entrepreneurs, and scientists. Although rare, stories of former foster children who became famous are nevertheless real. They inspire, motivate, and give hope. However, there is a higher probability of being struck by lightning than of spending childhood in foster care and ending up rich and famous.

CHAPTER EIGHT

Foster to Prison Pipeline

The foster to prison pipeline is a well-established trend showing that the foster care system is the number one supplier of residents to American prisons. The Juvenile Justice Information Exchange reported that, depending on location, between 25% and 70% of state prison inmates spent at least some time in foster care. Even the most conservative research indicates that within two years of leaving the system, about a quarter of former recipients of foster care will become involved with the criminal justice system. These numbers are alarming, and the reasons behind this phenomenon are known. Unfortunately, not many people care, and only a handful are invested in changing this trend.

Society generally looks down at children in foster care. Often viewed as troubled, many parents do not want their *good* children to socialize with foster kids. They are not welcome in people's houses because "What if they steal something?", "What if they set my place on fire?" or "What if they have a bad influence on my child?"

Children in general, and especially teenagers, are experts at getting into trouble. They have not yet developed mechanisms allowing them to control emotions. They turn little things into end-of-the-world drama, they scream, they fight, they talk back. What do we, as adults, do when it happens? We teach them. We patiently endure the abuse, and then we implement positive reinforcement: "If you behave, I will reward you." If it does not work, we try negative reinforcement: "If your shenanigans do not stop, I will take away your cell phone and ground you for a week." Does it work? Not immediately, and not always, but eventually, we turn our children into decent adults.

However, foster kids are not exposed to these parenting techniques. When a foster kid fights, foster parent calls 911, and the child is detained and perhaps incarcerated in a juvenile detention center. Foster parents are encouraged to follow this procedure. They are cautious with disciplining a foster child themselves because it may easily backfire, and they can be accused of abuse. Similar mechanisms can be observed in public schools. When a foster child is in trouble, he does not have a loving parent advocating for him. The principal picks up the phone and calls the police.

While the United States is engaged in a newly ignited debate as to whether or not racism or residual racism is still prevalent in our society, data clearly shows a disproportionate rate of school discipline targeting

African-American students. Maybe it is not racism, perhaps it is the lack of understanding of black culture among predominantly white school personnel, but the fact remains: black kids are more likely to be punished at school than their white peers.

A principal of a predominantly white school in a blue-collar suburb of Chicago was asked if his school has any African American students. "Yes, we do," he responded, "they are ALL in our program for students with emotional and behavioral problems." This interaction did not happen in the 1950s. It happened last year. And since black kids are twice as likely to be in foster care than white kids, they will be subjected to harsh discipline, frequently involving the police.

Educational data for the former recipients of foster care is grim. Although many qualified for tuition-free education at state colleges and universities, only a handful of current or former youth-in-care were able to take advantage of that opportunity. Former foster youth were eleven times more likely not to complete college than their counterparts representing the general population. One Midwest study, conducted by the University of Chicago, showed that only two-and-a-half percent of former foster youth earned a four-year college degree, compared to twenty-seven percent of young people from the general population. Former youth in care were twice as likely not to have a high school diploma or a GED.

About twenty thousand young people age out of the foster care system each year. For most, prognoses are not good. After being discharged, over ten percent of former youth in care were at some point homeless and forced to live on the streets or in homeless shelters. The percentage was higher for men than for women, but significant for both genders. Friends or relatives willing to offer a helping hand did not exist.

Three-quarters of the former recipients of foster care reported that they did not receive any type of employment counseling, and half never had training on how to apply for a job or write a resume. The US Department of Health and Human Services published a study analyzing employment outcomes for youth aging out of foster care over more than three years. The study covered California, Illinois, and South Carolina, and revealed that less than half of the former youth-in-care were able to earn an income at any time during that period. Thirty percent of youth in Illinois, twenty-four percent in California, and fourteen percent in South Carolina had no earnings at all. Those who worked earned significantly less than comparable groups of young people who never experienced foster care. Former-youth-in-care earnings placed them substantially below the poverty line.

Reports varied from year to year and from one region to another. Some indicated that up to forty-seven percent of the alumni of foster care were permanently unemployed. This data prompted some members of the US Congress to introduce an Improved Employment Outcomes for Foster Youth Act, which would allow employers to claim a tax credit up to $2,400 if they hire former youth in care who are below the age of twenty-seven. However, according to Congressional watch groups, the bill has no chance of being approved.

Children in foster care were removed from their homes for a reason – they were victimized and exposed to neglect, abuse, or both. They are more likely to develop PTSD than veterans. They need intensive therapy and a loving relationship with an adult who cares, but most of the time, they are deprived of both. Instead, they are heavily medicated, and as described in another chapter of this book, they are four times more likely to be prescribed psychotropic medication than other kids.

Girls in foster care are routinely targeted by sex traffickers. In fact, sixty percent of all child sex trafficking victims are, in some way, connected to the child welfare system. Girls are frequently coerced and later forced into prostitution. Yet, instead of helping them, we criminalize their behavior. By age nineteen, almost half of the girls and young women who graduated from the foster care system are pregnant. In the general population, that number was more than lower than half of that..

LGBTQ kids do not even have to come from foster care to be targeted for teasing, bullying, or worse. Now, imagine the fate of a black transgender kid, born as a male but identifying herself as a female, and being in foster care. That child will be rejected by almost every single group of society, including schoolmates, and frequently even foster parents. According to the Chronicle of Social Change publication, there is currently about two million homeless youth in the United States, and forty percent of them identify themselves as LGBTQ.

However, there appears to be a logical and straight-forward solution: over two million LGBTQ adults in the US are willing to foster or adopt a child. Yet, more than half of foster care agencies report never having placed a child with LGBTQ couples, and close to half would not even accept foster care applications from people identifying themselves as LGBTQ. For some reason, our society still believes that being gay is contagious, like a cold. We also think that if a gay foster child is placed with a heterosexual couple, that child will be *cured*.

After a foster child is detained or placed in juvenile detention, he rarely returns to a foster home. Usually, that child goes to a group home, and from then on, being arrested or detained becomes part of his daily routine. Life in a group home for foster youth with a juvenile record is described in my other book, "The Lost Boys from Longwood." Suffice to say that the group home to prison pipeline is wide open, with alumni of residential care being 2.5 times more likely to end up in prison than their foster home counterparts. By the age of seventeen, approximately ninety percent of kids who resided in group homes or who had more than five foster home placements have at least one arrest, conviction, or over-night stay in a correctional facility.

After reaching the age of eighteen, most foster kids age out of the system. One out of five kids become instantly homeless. They have no support, no family, no money, and no skills that would allow them to seek gainful employment. They have no health insurance, and no access to the psychotropic drugs that they are sometimes already addicted to. Many look forward to being arrested and sent to prison, where they are guaranteed three meals per day and a roof over their heads. In residential facilities for wards of the state, some residents meticulously plan to commit a crime immediately after discharge, which will ensure that they will go to prison. While groups of Christian and non-Christian activists loudly oppose abortion, children who were unwanted, neglected, and abused, and who grew up to be unwanted, neglected, and abused adults, are quietly moving from foster homes to park benches, and from park benches to prisons.

And America loves her prisons. More people are incarcerated in the United States than in any other country in the world, including Russia and China. The current population of the United States is approximately 330 million, and over 2 million are in prisons, not counting the almost 50,000 kids in juvenile detention centers. The United States incarcerates up to twelve times as many people as any other developed country. A quarter of the world's prison population is sitting behind bars in the US. For a former youth in care who suffers from mental disorders, is unemployed, has no permanent address, and no money to hire adequate legal representation, the chances of going to prison are high.

The American prison industrial complex is a lucrative business. The CCA, or Corrections Corporation of America (now CoreCivic), reported such excellent revenue that it became a publicly-traded company. Large financial institutions buy stocks of private prisons. Plus, prisons are not impacted by bad economies or fluctuations in international trade.

On top of that, many prisons provide cheap labor for corporations not directly involved with the prison industrial complex. A prisoner is paid anywhere between $0.12 and $0.40 per hour. There are no benefits that the company would have to pay, no unions, no unemployment insurance, and no workers' compensation. Companies are encouraged to hire prisoners and are offered tax incentives when they do. It is a perfectly legal modern slavery happening right in front of our noses, and its supported by politicians and lobbyists.

With many domestic factories gone or moved to countries that offer cheap labor, prisons are also a significant source of employment for people with limited qualifications. You put seventy-five percent of the local population inside a prison, you hire the remaining twenty-five percent to guard them, and the taxpayers will pick up the tab. It's perfect! To add insult to injury, some private prison companies have signed "occupancy guaranteed" agreements with the states. Based on these agreements, states must ensure that they will provide a certain number of prisoners so that a private prison has no vacancies. Otherwise, the state must pay a fee. To meet these requirements, states need criminals, and if they are not readily available, something can always be arranged, and the young people who have just left foster care are perfect for this role. After all, if we lock them all up, they will not be missed.

ACLU is sounding an alarm, warning us that we have created "a disturbing national trend," wherein foster children are funneled out of public schools and into the juvenile and criminal justice system. Still, nobody seems to listen. Unfortunately, our country is carrying a painful baggage of racism, classism, and xenophobia, and without putting those beliefs to bed and addressing poverty and inequality, there is little hope that the foster to prison pipeline will be shut down.

Over forty-eight percent of young adults who experienced foster care made a plan to commit suicide. Over thirty-seven percent actually tried to kill themselves.

CHAPTER NINE

Grady

Grady would tell you that he was born somewhere in the middle of twelve siblings. Nobody paid much attention to what Grady said because Grady was a master of tall tales. He would say that in his foster home, he had a huge flat-screen TV on each wall. Or that there was a secret passage to a cellar with medieval armors and ancient swords. Kids in the system sometimes do this because their reality is too sad to reveal. They feel compelled to imagine an alternative.

Everyone was surprised when they found out that Grady was number seven among thirteen kids. Most of his sisters and brothers had different dads, and his mom drank and used drugs. When Grady was little, nobody registered him in school. He never attended Kindergarten or the first grade. His education started in the middle of the second grade after he was taken by state protective services.

At that time, although Grady was new to school, he was already an expert on poverty. When he was no more than a toddler, his mom became homeless, and Grady and some of his brothers and sisters lived in a car. Grady did not remember how many, but he said that the old station wagon was crowded. Later on, his mom was able to rent a small apartment, but she was not supposed to live there with more than one child. Whenever their landlord knocked on the door, the kids were required to hide underneath the bed or go inside the closet or kitchen cabinets.

Once a day, his mom would take them to a supermarket and say, "Whatever you can grab without people seeing you will be your food for the day." For Grady, stealing food was both a way of life and a means of survival.

When Grady was eight-years-old, there were still seven children living in the apartment. The older ones left, and Grady never saw them again. He never met his grandparents, nor did he know what a grandparent was.

With seven kids still living with her, his mom eventually became overwhelmed. One day, which Grady would never forget, she lined up all of her remaining children and picked the ones she wanted to keep. Grady was not in that group. The five children who did not make it through the selection were taken to a cheap motel. The oldest was Grady's nine-year-old brother, and the youngest was a little over two. There were three boys and two girls. The mom told them to stay in the room and left. She never came back.

The kids were hungry, but they were used to it. At least, they had water. They even had a bed. Yes, they had to share it, but it still beat sleeping in a car. They stayed inside the room because that was what their mom told them to do. On day three, a motel employee found them and called the police. They were taken by the Department of Children and Family Services.

In the next eleven years, Grady went through twenty-three foster homes, two group homes, and one residential facility. Child Protective Services has a rule of not separating siblings, but when there are five of them, it becomes a daunting task to accomplish. The three youngest ones managed to stay together and later became adopted by the same family. Grady's older brother also ended up in a nice home and was adopted by a childless couple. But Grady had anger issues, attachment issues, stealing issues, lying issues, and more. For some unknown reason, the chaotic childhood had a more significant effect on Grady than on his siblings.

Unfortunately, Grady never found stability. On top of being an expert on poverty, he also became an expert on life in foster care. He would tell you that one of his foster homes was awesome, two or three were genuinely awful, and most were just OK. In the awesome one, there was a sweet Jewish couple that could not have children of their own. They worked relentlessly to bring Grady up to his grade level at school. They made sure he had everything he needed. They started a spectacular battle with the private foster care agency that handled Grady's case to make sure that he got the braces that he desperately needed. They loved Grady.

Grady might also admit that he was the one who blew this relationship. It was entirely his fault. No matter how much they begged him to stop, he continued stealing. He would do it whenever they took him to a store. To Grady, it was like second nature - something he could not resist. He also stole his foster mother's table set, which was a family heirloom, and he later destroyed it. He did not know why. They kept forgiving him, and they always believed his promise that he would never do it again. They would pay for damages, plead with store managers and police officers, and arrange private therapy on top of the therapy Grady was already getting through DCFS. Grady wanted to be good, but he couldn't control himself.

It was the increasing threats of physical violence that ended his future in that awesome foster home and obliterated his chances to be adopted. His foster mom became afraid of Grady. His foster dad wanted to keep him, but he was unable to ensure the safety of his wife. Therapy did not work, and Grady had to leave. The foster father begged to stay involved and – in some capacity – remain in Grady's life, but it was not allowed.

In the bad foster homes, Grady was dragged down the stairs by his hair. He was beaten with brooms, belts, cables, and bare hands. He would go hungry for days. There were chains with locks on refrigerators and pantry doors. When he complained to his caseworker, his foster parents denied all allegations, accused him of something preposterous, and kicked him out.

In the OK ones, nobody cared. Foster parents were not engaged in the lives of their foster kids. They would not have conversations; they were not interested in what foster children were doing or where they were going, with whom, and why. They were not in any way invested in a foster child's progress at school. If there was a problem, they would notify the agency and let the caseworker deal with it. Grady would say that they were not cruel or evil – they just did not give a damn. They were in it for the money.

This is Grady's life story. Today, he is a young adult without a steady job and without realistic prospects of getting one. He rents a room in a moldy and cold basement. He never reconnected with his siblings. He tried, but they were not interested anymore. He has a hard time building and maintaining relationships with females. He would like to have someone to love – in fact, this is all Grady wants – but he does not know how to make it work. For a while, wondered why he was even born and contemplated suicide. Eventually, Grady came to terms with his existence, although he is still unable to figure out its purpose.

CHAPTER TEN

Zach

When you walk across the Chicago financial district, you may wonder how many of the young homeless people who are panhandling on the street corners have recently graduated from the system of foster care. When Zach walks through this part of the city, he worries that he may soon have to join them.

Zach has recently turned twenty-five, and so far, life has not been good. He only vaguely remembers his childhood, and what he does remember is brutal and scarce. One thing he will never forget is his father throwing his little sister out of the second story window, only because she was crying when he wanted to watch TV. Zach ran to his neighbors for help and his dad never forgave him, but Zach's sister survived. There was an investigation. Zach and his siblings were taken by Child Protective Services.

Zach spent eleven years in foster care. He does not remember how many schools he attended; he lost count after ten. He bounced from one foster home to another. He was separated from his siblings and never stayed in one place long enough to make friends. He never connected with any of his foster parents. He spent countless hours in therapy, most of it utterly pointless. There was that one therapist – an older man named Wally - who understood Zach and who knew how to help. But Wally quit after getting a job as a director at some fancy private facility. Other therapists assigned to Zach were cute, young women, and Zach enjoyed his sessions because they were easy on the eyes. It was fun to tell them exactly what they wanted to hear and, from time to time, even make them cry. They were clueless. Zach felt like the king of bullshit.

His first arrest was an accident. Zach was only nine at the time. When he aimed a paintball gun at a passing squad car, he had no idea that the cop would roll down his window in that exact moment and get hit right above the nose. What are the chances, right? Well, the case did not even go to court. Zach had to wash the squad cars at the nearby police station for the entire summer.

In his sophomore year in high school, Zach fell in love with a girl named Rachel. At first, everything was perfect, and life was finally good, but then, Rachel had more and more things to do that did not involve Zach. He did not like that at all. If Rachel was his girlfriend, she was supposed to belong to him all the time and not just when she was available. So, Zach started taking her phone away and checking her text messages. A few times, he followed her to some of her personal things. Well, maybe more than a few. They eventually fought, and she attempted to break up with him. He grabbed her. Perhaps he was a little rough, but he could not remember the details. She ran home crying, her parents called the cops, and Zach was arrested.

More or less, the same thing happened again and again. After Rachel there was Kate, after Kate, there was Mandy, and after Mandy came Beth. When Zach turned eighteen, his visits to juvie were replaced by visits to the county jail. One time, Zach had to stay for over two months, officially earning him a criminal record.

Zach did not understand why his relationships always had turbulent endings. All he wanted was to have someone to love and someone who would love him back. He gave those women one hundred percent, he claimed. He belonged to them, and he had every right to expect that they belonged to him. But there was always something that pulled them away. To Zach, it was a matter of some primary loyalty. "Either you are with me, or you are with your mother. When you are with me, do not tell me that your mother wants you to do chores or that you have to babysit your little sibling. You are supposed to be with me and only with me. Your mother can make other arrangements. Can't you just tell her? And do not call the cops on me after I pushed you around. Couples fight. This is what people do, isn't it? You should have seen what my father did to my mom and to all of us."

Zach attended college for precisely two weeks, but after that, he had to quit. Was it because of Mandy? Or maybe Beth? Anyway, he had to be with his girlfriend and could not go to classes anymore. The same thing happened with all of his jobs.

A different set of problems came from Zach's habit of impersonating police officers and firefighters. Being a cop or a firefighter was always his dream. In high school, he even joined the Police Explorers program and worked hard to become the best in his group. Zach admired the respect invoked by those uniforms and envied the power that came with the job. Zach believed that the uniform would hide his emotional scars and change him into someone else – someone strong who was never a victim of abuse and who never experienced foster care. The only problem was waiting until this dream could become a reality and working to earn a degree. Waiting was never one of Zach's strong suits, and neither was work. Instead, he put on his Explorers' uniform and went out to an intersection close to his foster home to direct traffic. He was eventually detained by real cops and kicked out of the Explorers program. Severak months later, when he tried to be a cop again, Zach was arrested. The third time, he took a friend to a hospital wearing a firefighter's jacket. It created confusion, and Zach went back to jail.

Zach is currently living with another girlfriend. He has criminal record. He does not have a job. He has a high school diploma and some skills but no career. He has no car, no bank account, and no cell phone. His girlfriend, Nancy, is working full time and making enough for both of them, but they are barely surviving. Zach is spending most of his time at home. He has gained a lot of weight, probably from watching television all the time, but what else is there to do? He receives food stamps.

At this point, Zach is aware that he will never be a firefighter or a cop. Life is stressful, and Zach and Nancy fight a lot. Zach cannot look at himself in the mirror. He is a nobody. He cares about Nancy, but he is not always sure if she cares about him. What if she kicks him out? Where is he going to go? Zach can see no way out of this mess. He would like to know why his life had to turn out like this. He wants things to get better. He wants it so much that this need, this desire, eats him alive. He is desperately clinging to hope, but with age comes the realization that what you want is not what you are going to get. Zach is lost.

CHAPTER ELEVEN

Medicating Billy

Billy poured lighter fluid on his shorts and set himself on fire. While doing it, Billy laughed uncontrollably. Fortunately, Billy's foster mom did not panic, but quickly grabbed a bathroom towel and extinguished the flames. She reacted fast and Billy was not hurt. The only victim of his little pyromaniac escapade was Billy's shorts. All attempts to find out how Billy was able to get lighter fluid and a lighter were futile. His foster mom notified the agency, and Billy was taken to a mental hospital.

At the time of the incident, Billy was twelve. In his five-year career in the foster system, he moved from one home to another because nobody could handle his extreme behaviors. Billy was physically abusive toward other kids. He screamed, yelled, and threw tantrums on a regular basis. One of his favorite pastimes was trashing his room. He was a compulsive liar. Billy was also known for hurting himself, which made him a frequent visitor to an inpatient psychiatric facility for kids.

On top of all this, Billy exhibited a wide variety of medical problems. He complained about stomach pain all the time and would frequently throw up. He could not sleep. He had extreme mood swings, ranging from euphoria to irritability and depression. He developed allergies. His vision deteriorated and he was required to wear glasses, which he lost all the time. His weight increased, and so did the levels of his blood sugar. From time to time, Billy would say that he saw things that were not there, but with Billy and his constant lying, nobody knew if he was telling the truth.

Billy was on Risperdal and Ritalin. He took Melatonin and Amaryl. He also took something for his allergies, and due to his frequent colds and flu, he was prescribed antibiotics several times per year.

Billy did not have a regular pediatrician because, as a foster child, he was on a medical card, and no doctor around his foster home would accept it. When he had one of his frequent accidents, or when he was sick, Billy's foster mom would take him directly to the emergency room. ERs are not allowed to refuse patients, so Billy's caseworker advised his foster parents not to waste time trying to locate a physician who accepts Medicaid. Instead, they were told to go straight to an ER. In many states, this is routine procedure. A visit to a doctor would cost one hundred dollars, while a visit to the ER carries the cost of a thousand dollars or more, but that's all right.

Taxpayers are rich and enjoy paying ten times more for things that could cost less.

The agency had a contract with a psychiatrist that Billy would see once or twice a year. The visits were brief, usually lasting five to ten minutes, after which Billy would leave the doctor's office with a new prescription. Sometimes, when things with Billy were exceptionally bad, the caseworker would arrange prescriptions without even sending Billy to the doctor.

When Billy turned fifteen, he did something exceptional and unique for a kid in his situation: he briefly paid attention in class. During that fleeting moment, Billy learned that people, even teenagers, have the right to refuse medication. And that was exactly what Billy decided to do – he flat out refused to take his meds.

In a matter of weeks, Billy's health improved. In a few months, he lost weight and was able to participate in sports. He slept like a log, and he developed a great appetite. From time to time, to keep up with his well-established tradition, Billy would still trash something, yell, or threaten other kids, but overall, his behavior improved. His foster mom said that Billy cured himself by rejecting the benefits of modern medical knowledge.

On the other hand, little Gabriel Myers, a foster child in Florida, was not so lucky. Gabriel committed suicide. He hung himself on a shower hose that he wrapped around his neck. At the time of his death, Gabriel Myers was only seven years old. Like Billy, he exhibited extreme behaviors, and like Billy, he took a variety of meds. An investigation concluded that the excessive use of psychotropic drugs was a factor that contributed to Gabriel's death.

While addressing an opioid epidemic in our society, we must also finally admit that we have established a culture of over-medicating our children. Good parenting has been replaced by meds. In general, our kids are hyperactive. There may be several factors causing this phenomenon: maybe we do not spend enough time with them; maybe they eat unhealthy foods; perhaps it is a consequence of environmental factors, like too many video games, too much television, or too much violence in the world. Sometimes, parents do not know how to handle a naughty child and ask the pediatrician to prescribe meds as a solution. Frequently, the request for medication comes from school. School personnel are not qualified to make medical diagnoses, yet many teachers do. At a parent-teacher conference, they inform the mom that her child has ADD or ADHD. They tell the mom that if she wants the kid to be successful at school, she should make sure that her child gets proper medication. Some teachers would even tell the parent what should be prescribed and what would be the appropriate dosage.

The equation already looks bad, but let's throw another variable into the mix: a child in foster care. He is an African-American boy who has never experienced much parenting from his biological mom, who works hard on killing herself with meth. In his short life, the boy has been subjected to significant physical and psychological trauma. Eventually, he was removed from his unsafe home and placed in foster care. He now attends a predominantly white school where white teachers are not familiar with African-American culture. What in his previous, mostly African-American school, was considered a norm, now is viewed as a problem. Due to his past experience, the boy is acting out. He has a caseworker through foster care, a therapist, a psychiatrist, a CASA advocate. He has a case manager and a social worker at school. He also has a judge in a family court who periodically reviews his case. He seems to have an army of people working with him or for him, but he does not have one person he truly needs: a loving parent. What are this boy's chances of getting a prescription for psychotropic drugs? One hundred percent.

Nearly one in four kids in foster care take at least one psychotropic medication. While in the general population, the number is already alarming, among foster kids, it is four times higher. We prefer to medicate than to educate, and with foster children, this statement is even more true.

A foster mother recently posted a comment on social media, "My doctor said that my foster son was on twelve different meds when he was placed with me. My doctor got him down to three, and then to just one. Before, when he was taking twelve pills, my foster son was put in special education because he struggled at school. I have only had him for four months, but since we cut down his meds to one, he is doing regular school work and just made the merit roll. There was no need for all those meds, and I am not quite sure why he was on so many."

Another foster mom responded, "I refused to make my foster daughter take meds that were not working and made her not her. Caseworker and doctors were not impressed with my lack of forcing her, but I was equally unimpressed with their lack of effort to get to the root cause of the issue and instead just putting a band-aid on the symptoms."

That foster mother may call herself lucky. In many states, refusing to force medication on a foster child would result in removing the child from that home.

It is hard to imagine that the situation could be worse, but sometimes it is. Many foster children, deprived of regular and quality pediatric care, rely on sporadic visits to psychiatrists contracted by foster care agencies and pressured to prescribe psychotropic drugs. In some states, prescriptions are issued by nurse practitioners, and a foster child does not even see a doctor. Consequently, some children take a variety of different medications, which cause potentially opposing mechanisms. A good example of this is a combination of Ritalin and Risperdal, which was the case with Billy. While the first one is a stimulant that increases levels of dopamine, the second one is an antipsychotic, which blocks the effects of dopamine. This would be like taking a sleeping pill and drinking espresso at the same time. Nobody of a sound mind would do it. Yet, we are carelessly poisoning children in foster care with excessive and sometimes wrong medications. The obvious consequences are increasingly severe side effects. The child becomes even more unmanageable, bounces from one foster placement to another, eventually ages out of the system, and moves from the Ritalin/Risperdal cocktail to crack cocaine.

This phenomenon is not new. The consequences are well known. The doctors sound alarms. Yet, nobody listens. Nobody seems to care.

CHAPTER TWELVE

A Big Foster Ruffle

A middle-aged couple with solid moral standards, a nice income, and a comfortable home in a suburb of Chicago decided to open their doors and their hearts to a foster child. They believed they could have a positive impact, maybe even change the child's life. They contacted the state child welfare agency, attended twenty-seven hours of training, had their house inspected, obtained a foster parent license, prepared the room and… nothing. No child was placed with them. After three months of waiting, they grew anxious. After six months, they were furious. Why is the state calling for more foster parents, but when a couple actually goes through the entire checklist to become eligible, the state will not place children with them? Does the state need foster homes or not?

In fact, it is not that simple. In Illinois, foster care is based on a peculiar public/private partnership. This same model was introduced in the late 1990s by Kansas, followed by Michigan, Texas, Florida, and Georgia. It allowed for contracting private nonprofit agencies to supervise care in foster homes and arrange for adoptions. Private agencies provide direct supervision to foster children, while the state only oversees the process. Initial results were optimistic and showed a spike in numbers of adoptions, at least in Kansas. Multiple publications praised the model as revolutionizing the foster care system of the United States. Other states, including Illinois, followed suit.

Over the following decade, adoption data from Kansas was less optimistic and showed a significant fluctuation. For example, the number of adoptions increased between 2010 and 2011 but then dropped by almost twelve percent between 2012 and 2013. Experts began to consider that there were other factors at play. Some raised voices of criticism regarding how private child welfare agencies were paid.

In Illinois, while under contract with the state's Department of Children and Family Services, private agencies provide direct care to about eighty percent of foster children. Different private agencies are not equal, and some offer better services than others. If a couple obtains a foster parent license, but they do not reside within the service area of a certain private agency, a foster child may never be placed with them. Nowadays, it makes more sense to talk to a private agency first and arrange for a licensing process with them rather than to deal with the state.

No two agencies are alike, even though they all receive the same amount of money from DCFS to cover the foster care of each child. For example, on one foster child's birthday, a private agency gave him a cake mix that cost them less than two dollars. The same child was transferred to a different agency and, on his next birthday, received a Sony video camera worth over two hundred dollars. Similarly, while some private agencies may welcome involved and nurturing foster parents, others would turn them down because such parents would be too demanding. They would want all kinds of support and services, which the agency is not willing to provide. One foster father, who tirelessly advocated for his kid's medical needs, was told that he was "a nuisance to the smooth running of the system." "Smooth running" means not having any expectations and not asking the agency for anything.

Typically, crusaders are not welcome. Private agencies know how to spot a crusading idealist, and they try to discourage such people from fostering a child at the very beginning of the licensing process. Crusaders are considered nothing but trouble.

In general, obtaining a foster parent license through a private agency is not a pleasant or welcoming process. In one case, a husband and wife interested in opening their home to a foster child went through an initial interview with a director of a private child welfare agency located on a south-western suburb of Chicago.

"What job do you have?" asked the director.

"I own an auto body shop," responded the father.

"Really?" The director smiled knowingly. "A body shop... Is it because you like bodies? Do you prefer little girls' bodies, or maybe you enjoy little boys' bodies?"

While the father was instantly ready to punch the director in the face and deal with his first assault charge, he had to ignore the insults, or he would never see a foster child placed in his house. While talking with potential foster parents, private agencies have a lot of power, and some enjoy it too much.

Most private care agencies value foster parents who show a sort of professional detachment from their foster children. For years, foster communities in the Chicago area were retelling a horror story about a husband and wife and their two little foster girls. The wife could not conceive, and they were resigned to the fact that they would remain childless. On vacation in Colorado, they accidentally came across two little sisters who, due to some tragic circumstances, were just taken by the state protective services. The older girl was three, and the younger one had just started to walk. Both husband and wife instantly fell in love.

The couple started a painstaking process of bringing the girls to Illinois. The wife would fly to Colorado twice a month. They retained a private attorney in Denver. When things started to look good, they bought a bigger house in an excellent school district. They turned the back yard into an awesome playground, and they prepared two rooms worthy of little princesses. They obtained Illinois foster parent licenses. Finally, they brought the girls home on what they would later describe as the happiest day of their lives.

Based on procedures that are followed in Illinois, while still in the parent's home, the girls were placed in a private childcare agency's roster of foster kids. Ten months later, due to another procedure, which was described as a standard rotation, they were transferred to a different private childcare agency. The new agency removed the girls from their house and placed them in a different foster home with three other foster kids. The new foster home was located much closer to the agency's offices, which would save the agency time and money and make life more comfortable for the caseworker and other employees involved with the case.

The couple who brought the girls from Colorado went berserk. They moved heaven and earth to bring the girls back, but to no avail. The wife suffered a nervous breakdown and had to be hospitalized. "And all this craziness could be easily avoided if that foster mom were a true professional," commented a caseworker after retelling the story. "Professional" means "do not get emotionally involved and do not dare to love your foster child. Remember that you are only servicing them."

Sometimes, however, the opposite occurs, and the child welfare system has to deal with parents from hell. A veteran DCFS employee was called to her supervisor's office and told to personally process a placement of a child. This time, a private agency was not involved. A well-connected couple from Lake Forest, one of the most affluent suburbs of Chicago, contacted the governor of

Illinois, who was a close friend of a friend. That friend also happened to be a major donor. The couple asked for assistance in acquiring a foster child, so their request was processed immediately and outside of the established procedures.

The DCFS employee went to meet the couple in their house and was immediately stunned by what she saw. The couple lived in a real mansion surrounded by meticulously manicured grounds and with a smaller residence for their household employees located in the corner of the enormous back yard. A child placed in that environment would live in a fairytale.

The couple had a grown daughter who no longer lived with them and a son who had just left for an Ivy League college on the East Coast. They were aware that they could radically change some child's life. The wife had enough time on her hands to provide that child with proper guidance. The couple gave it a lot of thought. They eventually prepared a shopping list, which they presented to the DCFS representative.

They wanted a girl, five or six-years-old, pretty, and without disabilities. She had to be intelligent and eager to learn. They wanted the girl to be white, blond, and preferably with curly hair, but they would settle for straight. They would not tolerate a child who was fat. They definitely wanted blue eyes. They expected the girl to be very well behaved, obedient, and polite. She had to have good taste. They wanted her to be responsive to direction and to always do as told. They expected her to be appropriately grateful for the opportunity they were creating for her. They wanted the girl to show interest in classical music and visual arts. They wanted her to be sparkling clean and with excellent habits regarding her personal hygiene. Obviously, she would have to be in perfect health. It would be nice if she also spoke another language but please, no Spanish. Maybe French?

This one in a million opportunity was wasted because DCFS was unable to provide an appropriate child. If a child ends up in the system, that child is usually nothing like that imaginary girl described by the wealthy couple. Foster children are not obedient, and they are indeed not grateful – they are angry and scared, and emotionally damaged. They are not well behaved because they never had a chance to learn. They do not show interest in classical music because they have never even heard it. They know nothing about visual arts. Right after being placed in a new foster home, they will probably act out as if saying, "Look how bad I am! Are you sure you can handle me?" They are incredibly cautious with getting attached to someone because they were hurt in the past, and they do not want it to happen again.

Little angels who are hungry and cold and who thank you on their knees for providing them with a bowl of warm soup and a roof over their heads belong to fiction created by Charles Dickens rather than to the foster care system of the United States. Foster children want what all other children have, consider normal, and take for granted: a real home with a real mom and dad who love them. But it is this very thing that a foster child is denied.

A foster child can develop close bonds with foster parents and may eventually love them, but it can only happen after foster parents prove that they are worthy of love. It can occur after the foster parents demonstrate loyalty and enormous patience. It will be a slow process during which the foster parents are certainly tested, carefully watched, and assessed by a foster child.

Whoever wants instant gratitude should consider adopting a puppy.

CHAPTER THIRTEEN

Chloe

If anyone can be called a veteran of the foster care system, Debbie deserves the title. She has been fostering for several decades and, over the years, has opened her doors to almost seventy children in need.

Just five days after her thirtieth birthday, Debbie was in a severe car accident. She spent months in a hospital, followed by several more months of rehabilitation. She came out of that ordeal with a permanent disability. Despite a reconstructive surgery, Debbie's mobility will always be impaired. She can walk, but it is a challenge. Following her accident, Debbie qualified for Social Security disability. She was still in outpatient physical therapy, and collecting her disability checks allowed her to spend more time with her two small children.

Following the best tradition of till death do us part, Debbie's husband left soon after her accident. The disability checks combined with child support were not enough to support Debbie and the kids. To supplement her income, she started babysitting, which soon evolved into a private daycare. Debbie was good with the kids, she enjoyed spending time with them, and eventually one of the mothers asked why she wouldn't go for a foster parent license. Debbie thought it was a great idea, started the process, and a few months later had a kid placed in her house.

Over the decades, Debbie fostered all kinds of kids, from babies to teenagers, boys and girls, white, African American, and Hispanic. She developed strategies that allowed her to handle the foster care bureaucracy. She had good relationships with the caseworkers, and she smoothly maneuvered among the countless doctor's appointments, family court appearances, and IEP meetings. She fought to limit excessive medication, to increase therapy sessions, or, in some cases, to reduce them when a kid barely had time to do homework.

Over the years, Debbie has learned a lot about children. Based on her extensive empirical experience, she would say that kids go berserk during a full moon, and that they all lose their mind after home visits. But home visits are part of a deal. With two kids of her own, Debbie never planned to adopt. Her house was more like a Grand Central Station with kids coming and going all the time. For most children in foster care, the ultimate goal is reunification with biological parents. They are removed from the home due to neglect or abuse, but if parents can meet certain conditions, they will get their kids back. Before it can happen, children stay in a foster home and only see their parents during home visits. These visits are almost always traumatic, the kids come back to their foster home emotionally disturbed, and a foster parent must always deal with the aftermath.

If you are not planning to adopt, rule number one of fostering is not to get too attached to a child. Since they are not only children but children in need, they are easy to love. However, you must always remember that you only provide temporary care, room, and board. The child will be with you for just several months, but then, the child is inevitably going to leave. Keeping an emotional distance is necessary to maintain your own sanity.

However, this rule applies only to children and does not cover little angels sent to Earth to bring happiness and joy. And Debbie believes that Chloe was an angel. Although Debbie goes to church every Sunday, she does not consider herself a particularly devout Christian. Yet, Debbie was one-hundred percent sure that Chloe could not be a regular, human kid, because Chloe was too good and too precious. And so, despite her golden rule, Debbie fell in love with Chloe and was willing to go to Hell and back for that little girl.

When Chloe was first placed with Debbie, she was three-and-a-half. Debbie thinks that all children are beautiful and unique, but Chloe was something exceptional. First, she was unbelievably obedient. She did everything as told; she ate everything you put on her plate; she never fussed and never complained. Chloe probably did not know how to cry because she never did. She had wavy dark hair and huge blue eyes, which always looked at you with love and trust. Chloe was also unusual because she did not spend a lot of time in front of the TV. Whenever possible, she was outside looking at birds, chasing butterflies, or gently smelling flowers. Chloe was a little elf. She had a special connection with nature. She fed all the feral cats in the neighborhood, and she even befriended a wild rabbit.

Another unique thing about Chloe was that she could detect when you were sad or tired. When it happened, Chloe would come over to you, put her little hand on your forehead, and smile, maybe give you a kiss. "Believe it or not," says Debbie, "but I swear to God that little girl had healing powers."

Chloe's biological mom had schizophrenia and suffered an episode, after which Chloe had to be removed from her house. Chloe's dad was never identified. After having her daughter removed, Chloe's mom started taking her antipsychotic medication, made an outpatient commitment, and showed an excellent therapeutic response. She wanted Chloe back in her arms, as did the foster care agency. After a little over six months with Debbie, Chloe went back to live with her biological mom. Debbie's heart was broken, but she knew that that day would come.

Not even three months later, the caseworker called Debbie and asked if she would take Chloe again. The child's mother stopped taking her meds and had another episode. Nobody knew what happened, but Chloe ended up in an emergency room with injuries.

Of course, Debbie would take Chloe back. As far as Debbie was concerned, Chloe could stay with her forever. And so, Debbie's back yard turned into an enchanted garden again. Most feral cats were back, and so was the bunny. On bad days, Chloe's little hand on Debbie's forehead replaced Tylenol. Chloe's laughter filled the house. Even other foster children behaved better when Chloe was around.

Debbie knew that the agency planned to reunite Chloe with her biological mother again. It was like a déjà vu. Chloe's mom went to a mental hospital and started taking her meds. She was discharged and made a commitment that she would continue in an outpatient clinic. She had supervised visitations with her child. After another six months of treatment, her psychiatrist stated that she was ready to be permanently reunited with Chloe. This time around, the caseworker was hesitant, but the mom had a good lawyer, some hotshot from a large firm working pro bono on the case. After resisting for several months, the judge ruled that the child should be permanently reunited with her biological mom. Debbie's heart was broken once again.

Debbie and Chloe's next encounter was by pure chance, out of all places in a local Walmart store. Chloe was bigger but still on the small side, mesmerized by a Barbie doll in a shimmering gown. When she saw Debbie, she immediately ran to her with a big smile, yelling, "Aunt Debbie! Where were you, Aunt Debbie? Can I go home with you? Please, Aunt Debbie, please, take me home!" Chloe caused a scene, her mom and her male companion looked angry, and Debbie felt awkward. As gently as she could, Debbie explained to Chloe that she had to go home with mom. And once again, Chloe did as told, but for the first time, Debbie saw the pain in the child's eyes.

Following the incident, Debbie was restless. She called Chloe's caseworker to ask about the child but was told that the woman quit. She called the agency and asked if they were confident that everything was all right with Chloe and her mom. She was assured that the child was safe, and so was her mother, who was diligently taking her meds. There was no reason for concern. Debbie started regularly shopping in that Walmart, even though it was out of her way, but she never saw Chloe again.

Debbie's older biological child moved to the West Coast, the younger one graduated from college and also moved out of the house. More and more often, Debbie took in children with disabilities. Because she was disabled herself, she understood what they were going through. Getting a little more stipend money was also nice. She had a cute seven-year-old born with cerebral palsy. She also had a young, nonverbal man with autism and a cognitive disability, who was waiting for an opening in an assisted living facility where he would probably spend the rest of his life.

One day, the agency called and asked if Debbie was willing to accept a challenging case. A child was admitted to a hospital with multiple stab wounds. The child was stabbed with a large kitchen knife and sustained severe damage to the cervical spine. Consequently, the child became quadriplegic and had to be put on a ventilator. The prognosis for recovery was poor. The court was in the process of assigning guardian ad litem to decide the fate of the child. For now, they really needed someone experienced, and they wondered if Debbie was up for the challenge. After some hesitation, Debbie agreed.

After all the required medical equipment was set up in one of the rooms, an ambulance brought the child. Debbie went outside, looked, and thought she was going to faint. It was Chloe.

CHAPTER FOURTEEN

Mark

At the age of twelve, Mark had already experienced his share of foster homes. He lost count at some point, but there were at least fifteen. He rarely lasted in one for more than six months. Many foster parents said he exhibited maladaptive behaviors. Mark was in therapy all the time, but over the years, he developed a skill that allowed him to pretend to be engaged while mentally blocking all that therapy crap from his head.

Mark liked his current foster home. It was just him, his foster mom, Linda, and her biological son, Peter, only eleven months younger than Mark. Mark had nice clothes and all the food he could eat. He had a cell phone and an Xbox; he was on a baseball team and played hockey over the weekends. They even went on vacation in Florida, although his agency did everything humanly possible to prevent it. When you are in the system, they don't want you to leave the state. But Linda would not give up, and they went. Mark even bought a bunch of fireworks when they passed through Georgia. They were supposed to fire them on the Fourth of July, but Mark accidentally made them explode on a beach before the holiday, all at once, inside a cooler. The cooler was burned, and Linda joked that when Mark grows up, he will have to buy her a new one.

Linda obtained her foster parent license just for Mark, and only because he asked. Mark was tired of bouncing from one foster home to another, he needed a mom, and he decided that Linda should take the job. You cannot leave these things to chance, and you certainly cannot count on your caseworker. Mark knew that Linda cared. She was his middle school teacher and always made sure that he had everything he needed. When his foster parents did not make him lunch and forgot to give him lunch money, which was most of the time, Linda would invite Mark to share lunch with her. She was easy to talk to, and she knew how to listen. And so, one day at lunch, Mark summoned all of his courage and said,

"I have a big favor to ask, but I am afraid you are going to say no."

"What is it?" asked Linda.

"But do you promise that you will not say no?"

"Mark, what is it?"

"Will you please be my mom? Cause, you see, I could really use one..."

For some reason Mark could not understand, Linda seemed shocked and tried to convince Mark to make things work in his current foster home. But after he was kicked out and moved to another place again, she changed her mind. She got licensed, and although it took a long time, Mark ended up with Linda and Pete.

With Linda, Mark finally had a chance of being adopted. Linda made him a promise, and when Linda said something, she made sure that it happened. They just had to wait a little longer. Mark knew that in Illinois, you must live in a pre-adoptive home as a foster kid for a year before the courts will proceed with an adoption, but Mark didn't mind. Life was good, and Mark was finally able to breathe.

And then, out of the blue, his agency removed Mark from Linda's place and put him in a different foster home. Once again, everything changed in the blink of an eye. Mark was kicking himself in the butt for letting his guard down and having a moment of hope. For someone in the foster care system, hope is a dangerous thing.

Mark's agency was not evil, nor did his caseworker hate him. It was just a matter of efficiency. Rather than driving for over an hour one way to conduct a required monthly visit with Mark at Linda's place, the caseworker could now do it in less than ten minutes and service four foster kids at the same time. The new foster home was located close to the agency. The agency was working toward improving efficiency, and moving Mark was a business decision. Destroying Mark's only chance for being adopted was just an unfortunate side effect.

There were other private child care agencies located close to Linda's place. Theoretically, Mark could have been transferred to any of them, but his agency would not have it. Why would you voluntarily get rid of a kid who brings you at least fifty thousand dollars per year? It would be a horrible business decision. So, Mark ended up in a home with three other foster kids and three adults with severe mental impairment placed there by the Department of Human Services.

With seven people under her care, Dannisha, who was Mark's new foster mom, should have had her hands full, but that was not the case. She was never there. She loved gambling and spent most of her days and almost all nights in a nearby casino. Usually, this was fine. Her foster kids were all teenagers and could take care of themselves without someone hovering over their heads. Plus, there were really just three of them because Tanika, the only girl in the group, disappeared. Maybe she ran away, or perhaps something happened to her, but the foster mom forbade anyone to say anything and did not file a report. In case the agency called or a caseworker came by, they were supposed to say that Tanika got detention and had to stay at school. In case the school called, they were supposed to say that the agency took Tanika for an extended home visit. Otherwise, DCFS would stop paying for Tanika, and that was something Dannisha simply could not allow.

On the other hand, the disabled people who lived in the house were not interested in Tanika, her disappearance, or her whereabouts, because they were not aware of what was going on. A bus would take them in the morning and bring them back in the afternoon. After that, they would just stay in their rooms.

The house was a mess except for the living room, which was off-limits and used only for the caseworker's visits. There was usually food in the fridge, so nobody went hungry. If they were thirsty, they were encouraged to drink tap water. The only real problem was with the disabled people, who smelled so bad it was hard to be in the same room. From time to time, one of the foster kids could not stand it anymore and washed them, but Dannisha never did because she was never available. She was always at the casino. Having four foster kids and three disabled adults provided Dannisha with a steady income in the form of stipends, which amounted to over one hundred thousand dollars per year. Tax-free. With no work. However, most of the stipend money was swallowed by slot machines.

Meanwhile, Linda and Pete were told to break all contact with Mark. A therapist from his agency called and explained that staying in touch would have a negative impact on Mark's well being, and that continuing any kind of a relationship would be ill-advised. Seeing Mark was out of the question. He could develop attachment, and to those children, attachments were unhealthy and could result in emotional trauma. Would Linda want Mark to be even more traumatized after everything he went through in his life? Was she that selfish? The therapist explained that after all, he was a professional and knew what he was doing. Linda should follow his advice. The agency was acting in the best interest of those kids.

It was just an unfortunate fact of reality that some of the kids had to be frequently moved. The agency adopted a policy of clear-cuts with foster parents and starting anew.

Mark, Linda, and Peter did not listen to the therapist and stayed in touch. However, their interactions were now limited to phone calls. Linda continued with her efforts to adopt Mark.

Mark's new neighborhood was not famous for a good safety record. One day, when he was walking home from school, Mark was jumped by a bunch of boys. They stole some of his things and beat him up pretty badly. His nose was bleeding, one of his eyes was swollen shut, and he had cuts and bruises everywhere. He barely made it home. His foster mom was in the casino, so he called Linda for help.

Linda told Mark to clean the cuts the best he could, to contact Dannisha, and ask her to come home immediately and take him to a doctor. He called but had to leave a message. Two hours later, when Dannisha did not return his call, Mark contacted Linda again. She told him to keep trying. The foster mom was not answering and Mark was in pain.

Linda's first instinct was to drop everything and run to help the kid, but that would jeopardize her chances to adopt him. His agency was clear: no direct contact with Mark was allowed. Linda waited until midnight, but after that, she finally had enough and decided to call the DCFS hotline. She said that she was a mandated reporter and would like to report a case of neglect. A minor child had been injured and urgently needed medical assistance. His only caregiver was not home and could not be reached.

"Where is the caregiver?" asked the person taking the report.

"It is my understanding that she may be in a casino and is not answering her phone," explained Linda.

"Does she do it a lot?"

"Based on what I am hearing," Linda was careful with selecting her words, "she is usually gone all nights, comes home around five in the morning, and then sleeps for most of the day."

"Really? It must be hard on the kid. Do you know the name of the parent? Who is in charge over there? And how are you involved?" the person on the line sounded concerned.

"Well, YOU are in charge," said Linda. "He is YOUR ward, and I am his former foster parent who is also trying to adopt the kid. Somebody needs to take him to a hospital, and I want you to tell me how it will be arranged. Because if you don't, I am going to drive over there myself, and after I do, I don't want to hear from anyone that I had no right!"

The voice on the phone became distant.

"Well," he said, "if that child's foster parent is coming home at five in the morning, then technically, you cannot say that she is gone all night. She is back at five, isn't she? What is the address? We will take care of everything. Stay out of it and do not interfere."

Eventually, Mark fell asleep. Nobody took him to a doctor. Nobody checked on him. Dannisha came home in the morning and told Mark to put a compress on his swollen eye, attach band-aid to his cuts, and stop acting like a baby.

Later that day, Dannisha was contacted by DCFS. They told her that somebody filed a report stating that she was neglecting the kids and leaving them unsupervised. Dannisha was told to be home on Saturday between eleven and noon because DCFS was going to send someone to her place to check whether she was home. They also wanted to talk to the kids.

Dannisha was furious. She corralled the boys and told them what to say to DCFS. If anyone even mentions the word *casino,* he will be really sorry! If DCFS asks about Tanika, the boys were supposed to say that she was on a volleyball team and had to go to a game. Dannisha also told Mark that she knew it was him. He was to say that she took him to a doctor and that his former foster mother's report was nothing but lies. Dannisha warned Mark that if he even hinted that she was leaving them home alone, she would call the police and tell them that he was stealing from her. She would make sure he ends up in juvie.

On Saturday, the DCFS investigator showed up on time. He talked to the boys who ensured him that Dannisha was taking excellent care of everyone and that she would leave the house only to take them to appointments or buy food. The investigation was quickly closed. Things went back to normal. The flow of the taxpayers' money to the casino was restored. Linda was told to shut up and back off. Several weeks later, Tanika was finally reported missing. She was never found.

CHAPTER FIFTEEN

Victim of Santa Muerte

Oscar's earliest memory is that of being rich. His had a large condo in LA, in a neighborhood that was considered dangerous, but still, Oscar's family was always safe and well-respected. His dad told him that nobody would ever touch their family. Oscar knew that his father was someone important. They had expensive furniture, leather couches, and mirrors in golden frames. There were huge TV sets with surround sound speakers. There was also dad's drum set, but the kids were not allowed to touch it.

Oscar's father emigrated from El Salvador when he was a young kid. He came with nothing. However, his dad was smart and resourceful and climbed to a high position in an "organization." Now Oscar knows that the "organization" was, in fact, a gang, but back then, he had no idea. Sure, his dad looked a little scary. He had a lot of earrings and tattoos all over his body, even on his face. The tattoo of Santa Muerte on his chest was especially frightening, but he always told Oscar not to be afraid. Despite that somewhat terrifying appearance, Oscar believed that his father loved him. His dad said that others should be afraid, and that Oscar, his mom, and his baby-brother, Eduardo, will always be protected.

Oscar's mom was beautiful. She had light skin, long, raven-black hair, and big, almond-shaped eyes. His dad used to say that every man would like to be with Oscar's mom, but nobody would even dare to look at her.

They had everything they needed and more. Oscar believed that his parents loved each other, and they both loved him and Eduardo. Whenever his dad was home, Oscar would get anything he wanted. For a time, Oscar thought that his life was good.

Now, he knows better. He knows that by no means was his childhood good or normal. For example, when he was only seven, his dad took him to "work" to watch the execution of a man. The man was beaten to death with a baseball bat. Oscar's dad said that the man deserved it because he was a traitor and a thief. He also said that it was time for Oscar to start learning because someday, very soon, his associates were going to become Oscar's family.

As much as Oscar would like to say that he was traumatized by watching a man being brutally murdered, it would be a lie. He wasn't. His dad said it was normal, something that needed to be done, and Oscar never questioned his dad. Years later, Oscar started wondering if accepting that murder so easily made him a psychopath, which was a thought that terrified him. However, his indifference could also have a different explanation. Maybe children just accept the things that their parents tell them because children do not know the difference between right and wrong.

Oscar's favorite story was that of a boy who was the son of an Italian mafia hitman in Rhode Island. The story took place in Providence, back when the mafia was still in charge. The boy often watched his father whack people and put them into cement shoes to dispose of the bodies. Then, one day, the city of Providence installed a sidewalk on the street in front of their house. And they boy cried because so much concrete was wasted with nobody in it. Yes, children are easily manipulated. Oscar could definitely identify with that mafia boy.

Oscar's world crumbled after his dad left his mom. Oscar never knew what happened, but according to his mom, a younger model replaced her. To say that his mother could not accept rejection would be a gross understatement. Oscar's mom completely and entirely lost it. She yelled, screamed, wailed, and smashed everything they owned. She was constantly either drunk or high. One night, she grabbed a large kitchen knife and went after Eduardo, yelling that she was going to kill "that bastard's brood." Oscar was never so scared in his life, yet he tried to protect his little brother. He failed. His mom was not his mom anymore. She was crazy, she had Eduardo's blood all over her, and she was screaming that Oscar was next. Somehow, he managed to escape.

He ran to the street, jumped in front of a passing car, and told to the driver to call 911 because his mom had just killed his little brother.

When the cops showed up, Eduardo was still alive, but he died in the hospital a few hours later. The mother was arrested, and Oscar was taken in by strangers. It was all like a bad dream. It was as if Oscar stepped out of his body and was watching a scary movie that had nothing to do with his real life.

Oscar was eventually taken in by Grandma Gabriela. She was someone he knew and could trust, and he finally felt safe again. A few days later, his father showed up and hugged him and said that he was going to take Oscar and that Oscar will live with him and his woman. Later that night, in the kitchen, his dad had a loud argument with Grandma Gabriela. It was in Spanish, and Oscar could not understand everything they said, although he knew it was about him. The next morning, Grandma Gabriela packed a suitcase and took Oscar to stay with her friend. A week later, they were on a plane to Chicago. Oscar never saw his father again.

Life in Chicago was hard. They had a small apartment full of *cucarachas*. For a while, Oscar did not even have his own bed and had to sleep on a mattress on the floor. Grandma Gabriela was from El Salvador, like his mom and dad, but for some reason that Oscar did not understand, she avoided other Salvadorians. All of their neighbors were Mexican. Oscar was not allowed to say where his family was from.

His grandma worked, but she did not make much money. She always put food on the table, but the times of expensive toys and video games were long gone.

Eventually, Oscar adjusted to his new life. He made friends at school, and teachers liked him because he always came prepared and had good grades. Grandma Gabriela was obsessed with his schooling and would not even let him watch TV until he finished all of his home-work. Oscar, now a pre-teen, still had nightmares about his little brother being killed by his mom. However, his grandma would not let him talk about it, and he was strictly forbidden to ever mention his mother. Grandma told him to try very hard to forget. He knew he had aunts and uncles back in LA, but she would not give him their phone numbers and would not let him talk to any of them.

Another disaster struck when Grandma Gabriela was diagnosed with Alzheimer's. Grandma was old: Oscar's mom was her youngest child, born when grandma was almost forty. Oscar never thought that one-day, grandma might be unable to take care of him. He assumed they had plenty of time, but he was wrong. Grandma's Alzheimer's was aggressive and she was soon forced to go to a nursing home. A nursing home is not a place for children. Oscar was left all alone in the world.

He was placed in a foster home. His foster mother was black, and she was a devout Christian. One thing she hated more than anything was Catholics. And Oscar was a Catholic, always diligently attending mass with Grandma Gabriela, going to confession, and praying to

Virgin Mary. His foster mom found and threw away the rosary his grandma gave him on his birthday. His foster mom yelled at him, saying if he wanted to have a chance for salvation, he should convert to Christianity. Oscar did not budge. He yelled back. His foster mom accused him of stealing, and he was removed.

Oscar's next foster parent was a white man on disability who could not care less about religion. The only rule in his house was not to bother him unless there was an emergency. He spent most of his time watching television. Oscar and his foster brother, a white teenage boy staying in the same house, were expected to take care of themselves. All things considered, Oscar's new foster father was not bad. He was certainly better than the crazy Christian woman before him. But Oscar felt lonely. He needed someone close, someone he could love.

Her name was Lauren, and she was Oscar's first real girlfriend. She was blond, beautiful, popular, and nothing like the one-night-stands and *friends with benefits* that Oscar occasionally dated before. Soon, Lauren became Oscar's entire world, and there was absolutely nothing he would not do for her. For two beautiful months, Oscar was in heaven, and then, Lauren dumped him for a football player. To make it worse, she dumped him right after Grandma Gabriela died in the nursing home. Lauren said that if Oscar needed to talk about how much he missed his dead grandmother, he should go and find himself a shrink. Lauren had better things to do.

Oscar started to believe that he was cursed. He lost everyone he ever loved. He was left all alone and had no place in the world. He could see no future, and the pain was too much to bear. So, Oscar decided to end it all. He tried to hang himself, and he used Lauren's scarf as the rope. Fortunately, fate was not on his side, and the tree's branch that was behind his foster father's house broke. Oscar survived and was taken to the psych ward.

He was there for five months. He was supposed to be discharged after a little over a month, but the agency could not locate another foster home for him, so he just stayed there. It was like being in prison without committing a crime. The days dragged. During the nights, he could hear other kids screaming or crying. There was nowhere to go and nothing to do. They gave him medications even though he didn't want to be drugged. He believed that the drugs and alcohol were what made his mother kill Eduardo, so Oscar never touched them. He never even tried to smoke a cigarette or weed. In the hospital, he quickly figured out how to cheat and hide the pills underneath his tongue, only to spit them out after the personnel checked if they were swallowed.

As bad as it was in that mental hospital, at some point during his stay, Oscar made a decision that turned his life around. He was thoroughly tested, and a doctor, more specifically a psychiatrist, told Oscar that he had exceptionally high IQ. Oscar always knew he was smart; he received good grades without much effort, and it was easy for him to remember things. It also helped that he liked his shrink and actually listened to him. His shrink told him, "I will not treat you like a child. Either you are going to grow up, be a man, and take advantage of that big brain of yours, or you are going to keep feeling sorry for yourself until there is nothing left." The doctor also brought him a present: *The Chamber* by John Grisham.

The Chamber was the first of many books Oscar read in that hospital and discussed with his shrink. It started with Grisham but later included Hemingway, Steinbeck, Melville, Dickens, and even Dostoyevsky. The books transported Oscar to different times and different worlds. He realized that he was not the only person in the world who suffered, and he discovered that sometimes suffering would stimulate creativity. Literature became Oscar's new salvation. He suspected that he inherited this intellectual capacity from his father, who probably used his brains to achieve a high rank in the gang. But Oscar had other plans.

Finally, Oscar's agency found another foster home willing to take him. It was a single woman, Hispanic, and a retired teacher. She had originally stopped taking in foster children, but Oscar's shrink knew the woman personally and vouched for him, and she ended up taking him in. It was a quiet home, just with Ms. Sanchez, Oscar, and two raven-black cats. Oscar spent most of his time studying. He took AP classes and made an honor roll. Whenever he asked for assistance with homework, Ms. Sanchez was there to help. Until one day, when he was stuck on a calculus problem, she said, "The apprentice superseded the master. I don't know how to help you. You are on your own." But they remained close. They shared a passion for old movies, which they watched together over the weekends whenever Oscar was home, which was not often. Oscar was involved in a bunch of school activities. He was a member of a National Honors Society – one of only two Hispanics in his school. He was also the vice-president of a local chapter of Best Buddies, an organization of students that help kids with special needs.

For Oscar, going to college was the easiest thing in the world. With his grades, the community college was happy to have him. Plus, for a ward of the state, it was tuition-free. After earning his associate's degree, Oscar plans to transfer to a public university and go for a Bachelor's and then, maybe a Master's. He majors in psychology. He has already aged out of the system, but Ms. Sanchez has told him that he can stay in her house for as long as he likes.

Oscar finally understands why his grandma brought him to Illinois: to get away away from his father and the rest of the family. Oscar believes that his father truly loved him. Several times, Oscar was tempted to reach out and re-establish contacts with his relatives back in California, but then he thought better of it. Oscar feels that his father could always find him but made a decision not to. If Oscar could have a brief conversation with his dad, he would like to say, "Thank you."

Oscar is going to be in the elite group of only 3% of people who went through foster care, yet managed to earn a college degree. When asked if he had advice for others who were in the same predicament, Oscar smiled and said, "Wait until I get that degree in psychology. Maybe then, it will be easier for me to explain."

CHAPTER SIXTEEN

Emily

Emily was first sexually abused when she was nine. At that age, she had already experienced poverty, hunger, and abuse. She lived in a decaying house where everything was always broken and where you were lucky not to find roaches in the kitchen, bathroom, or in your bed. She shared her bed with a colony of bed bugs. Her mom did not do much cleaning because she was usually drunk, and her dad was come-and-go. Emily and her younger siblings definitely preferred when he was not there. Whenever he showed up, he drank with the mom and then beat her and the kids. For a while, Emily had a dog, Benji, whom she loved with her whole heart and who loved her back. It was a small mutt, and not particularly attractive, but one should not judge a dog by its look. To Emily, Benji was an angel.

One night, after several hours of drinking, the dad started slapping Emily's mom and Emily told him to stop. He went berserk, kicked Benji, and then hit him with an empty bottle several times. Benji was squealing, bleeding, and could not move. The dad dragged him outside and shot the dog with his rifle. Emily had to watch. He said that if she ever talked back to him again, she would be next. Then, he made her dig a hole with a shovel and bury the dog.

After Benji died, nobody loved Emily again.

When she was nine, her dad took her to some old guy Emily did not know, and she was raped. She hated it, she cried, and she begged her father to make it stop, but he just told her to shut up. She was in so much pain that she could not get up from the bed, and her dad had to carry her to his truck. The next day, she could not walk.

The second time was maybe a month later, but before it happened, she was forced to drink half a bottle of vodka. It was the worst thing she ever tasted, and after the first few gulps she threw up, but her dad made her finish the whole glass. After that, everything was a blur, and the only thing Emily remembered was that this time there were two guys..

This became a routine. Her dad would show up, make her drink, and then take her somewhere to have sex with old guys. Sometimes, it was in a home or an apartment, and sometimes, in a cheap motel. The only good thing was that her dad was nicer to her, and from time to time, he would even give her presents, like a bar of chocolate or a stuffed animal.

By the time she turned twelve, Emily was an alcoholic. When there was booze in the house, she would drink it by herself, with mom, or with both of her parents. Trips to dad's "friends" happened on a regular basis. Emily frequently ditched school, but nobody cared. Her dad did not beat her much anymore. He even bought her clothes and makeup, and he told her that she looked great. Emily was skinny and smaller than most girls in her class, but she had long, naturally blond hair, blue eyes, and freckles. Her dad and his "friends" enjoyed taking pictures of her without clothes. They liked doing other weird things to her, but by now, Emily was used to it. She learned how to turn things to her advantage and would tell dad that she was going to do what they wanted, but only after he buys her stuff. He usually did.

It all ended after one of her dad's "friends" was really rough and left Emily with cuts and bruises. She stayed home for two days, but when she did return to school, her teachers noticed. She was sent to the principal, who immediately called someone. Child Protective Serves eventually showed up. Emily was put in a foster home, and her dad was sent to jail.

The first foster home lasted for less than a month. They kicked her out after they found her drunk. The second one had no alcohol, but they wanted her to follow a litany of crazy rules: fold your clothes, clean your room, wash the dishes, take out the trash… "Don't you know how to do it?" No, she did not know because nobody showed her. She was never required to do any of those things before, but when she tried to tell them, nobody believed her. Also, without access to booze, she did not feel that great. She frequently yelled and trashed a few things a couple of times. Eventually, they kicked her out as well, although she made progress because that foster home lasted for more than three months. Her next foster home was a little better because nobody cared about what she did. There were two older foster kids over there who introduced her to weed, and later to stronger stuff. Not having access to booze was not so painful anymore.

Emily went to a lot of therapy. They told her that what her dad did to her was wrong and that none of it was her fault. They kept asking Emily about her feelings. They taught her what to do when she was really angry or upset, which helped a little but not much. However, she really liked the attention. They also told her that she should build a relationship with her mom, and that they should discuss what happened. Emily saw her mom from time to time, and she did what her therapist advised, but her mom just said, "Oh, stop being such a drama queen. It's time to grow up. How do you think I was making money to feed you?"

Her dad was released from jail because he denied everything, and there was no proof. However, he had to promise that he would stay away from the house and would not attempt to interact with Emily or his younger daughters. For a while, he kept that promise, but of course he returned at some point. He hid in the basement and the shed. Emily's mom told her that if she ever wanted to see her again, she had to keep quiet. And she did. She tried not to think what her dad was doing to her younger sister, Angela, who just turned nine.

Emily was thirteen when she was kicked out of her third foster home. It happened after her foster mom walked into the room when Emily was in bed with a boy. Emily pleaded with her and said what her mom had told her: not to be such a drama queen. Nobody listened, and Emily was out.

Emily was put in a group home. There was a lot of fighting among the kids, but Emily knew how to throw a punch and quickly earned their respect. In some ways, it was better than a foster home – nobody was on your back all the time. But Emily was growing up, and she wanted to have all the nice things that the other girls in school had. Unfortunately, nice things cost money, which was something that Emily did not have. In a group home, residents usually got a pitiful allowance, but even that would be taken away for misbehavior. For Emily, that meant her allowance was permanently withdrawn.

One day, when she was outside, a man approached her and asked if she wanted to make an easy twenty bucks. Of course she did. He took her to a motel and told her to have sex with a man. Piece of cake – this is what dad taught her to do a long time ago. Afterward, the man drove her back to her group home and asked if she would be interested in a little partnership. She said that she would. Soon, their business was booming. The guy, Bob, made arrangements almost every day, and Emily could finally afford to buy all the nice stuff that she always wanted.

Fate intervened less than a year into Emily's prosperous partnership with Bob. Emily was told that she would be going to another foster home. To make it worse, she was placed with a minister and his wife; both prudes and both crazy about God and other religious stuff. All they had in that house were rules, rules, and more rules. They treated Emily like a little girl. She was not even allowed to wear makeup. Her new school was awful. The minister's wife was home all the time, making sure Emily did her home, and she always made sure Emily made it to school. Emily kept asking her caseworker to move her someplace else – anything would be better than this house – but the caseworker said that the home was perfect, and that Emily must stay.

One thing that Emily managed to keep and hide from the reverend and his holy wife was a cell phone. From time to time, she talked to Bob. He told her how much he missed her and how wonderful it would be if she just moved in with him full time. With her looks, he told her, she could become a star. She could make a fortune being a high-priced companion to rich guys. Who knows, maybe someone in the business will notice her, and she will become an actress or a professional model.

So, Emily ran away. One day, after flunking a math test, storming out of the classroom, serving detention, and having another fight with the reverend, Emily called Bob and told him to pick her up. He was there in less than half an hour. Emily was fifteen and ready to become rich.

Things did not happen the way Bob described. There were no wealthy businessmen. Instead, there were more cheap motels and old, fat, sweaty men. Nor did Bob live in a mansion. He had a shabby apartment in a bad part of town that reminded Emily of her childhood home, and this was not the only similarity to Emily's childhood. After supposedly missing her so much, Bob was not exactly prince charming. He yelled and slapped her around, always complaining that she did not bring in enough cash. He became a spitting image of her dad. At least, they would not produce offspring. After what happened to her when she was little, Emily was infertile.

At the age of seventeen, Emily already felt old. Her life was a constant struggle, almost entirely devoid of happiness. She finally found the courage to leave Bob, and for the first time, she was on her own. She reached out to her mother, but there was no home to go back to. Her sister told Emily that her mom was almost permanently drunk, and that her dad was nearly always home. She wanted to ask Angela if her dad was doing to her what he did to Emily, but she did not. She was afraid that she might hear something she did not want to know.

And so, Emily was seventeen and homeless, with no skills, no high school diploma, and with nobody to lean on. She knew that she became a cheap hooker, but she did not know how to be anything else. She supplemented her income by panhandling on a street corner.

This has been Emily's life for the past six years. She is still homeless. She is now also addicted to heroin. Emily knows that she is killing herself, but she does not care.

Her life has been one big mistake anyway. She does not look good anymore. She is twenty-three-years-old, but she looks like an old woman.

When asked about her dreams, at first, Emily said that it was a stupid question and that she did not have dreams anymore. But after a few days, she said, "If someone could truly love me for just one day…" Emily also said that she knew she was going to die soon, and that when it happens nobody will miss her. Nobody will even notice. Maybe the city will bury her in some cheap grave with no name, and her worthless existence will be erased. But in a way, she says, she is looking forward to it. She knows that Benji is waiting for her by the rainbow bridge, and she will finally be loved again.

CHAPTER SEVENTEEN

Foster House of Horrors

Placing children in foster homes is not always the right solution. In Arkansas, foster parents Richard and Martha Roesch were arrested on charges of child abuse after they allegedly stabbed an adopted kid with a fork and shocked a little girl on her private parts with a cattle prod. There were also reports that they forced foster kids to wear plastic bags, sleep on tarps on the floor, and use buckets for a bathroom.

In Utah, foster parents Matthew Earl Waldmiller and his wife, Diane, adopted three boys from the state foster system. They made the boys sleep on the floor in a room without a light bulb and with the only exterior window painted black and screwed shut. The boys, who were between the ages of seven and eleven, spent close to thirteen hours a day locked in that room. According to news reports, when they complained or exhibited behaviors that their foster parents did not approve of, they punished the boys by forcing them to eat rice heavily seasoned with salt and cayenne pepper. At times, they were bounded with zip ties or had their mouths and eyes covered with duct tape. At the trial, the couple explained that they felt overwhelmed. While sentencing them to fifteen years in prison, the judge said that they "lacked human decency."

In Wisconsin, Dominique Lindsay fostered a baby boy who was only a few months old. A surveillance camera recorded Dominique yanking the baby from a car seat by his arm and carrying him – also by his arm – across the room. When the baby was taken to a hospital, doctors discovered multiple broken bones and torn flesh in his mouth. Dominique explained that the kid simply got on her nerves.

These cases may seem shocking, but they are not unique. The media reports similar stories every day. Children who were neglected and abused, and therefore removed from the care of their biological parents, are sometimes placed in foster homes where they become subjected to even worse neglect and abuse. Occasionally, atrocities committed in foster homes are so monstrous that they draw national attention.

Few cases were more shocking than the events that took place in the foster house of horrors ran by Judith Leekin. The widely publicized story started in Queens, New York, but later moved to Florida, where in 2007, the police found a disabled eighteen-year-old girl abandoned in a supermarket. The girl led them to the house of her adoptive mother, Ms. Leekin.

Using different aliases, Judith Leekin fraudulently adopted eleven children with disabilities ranging from autism to blindness. When the police finally entered the house, only ten children and young adults were alive. Eleven-year-old Shane Graham, who suffered from autism, Down's Syndrome, and sickle-cell anemia, vanished without a trace and was presumed dead.

All the children were beaten, caged, handcuffed, denied food and access to a toilet, tortured, and threatened with a gun. None of them attended school, and only three could read or write. They were locked in and forced to spend most of their lives indoors. They never went to a dentist or a doctor. Those who could talk told a story about a little girl with an intellectual disability who pulled decaying teeth from her mouth. One autistic boy was blind, possibly as a result of never being exposed to natural light. All children were covered with scars and had missing teeth. They were all close to starvation. Their adoptive mother, Judith Leekin, who is now serving a lengthy prison sentence, collected over one-and-a-half million dollars worth of subsidies from the state of New York. This allowed her to live a lavish lifestyle and move to a beautiful house in Port St. Lucie, Florida. By moving out of New York, she was also able to escape the oversight of the child welfare agencies that were assigned to watch over her adopted children.

Some say that the foster care system is broken and beyond repair. There are voices that claim it might be better to return to the old model and put children in orphanages, where they would at least be fed and feel safe. Even some of the people who went through the system of foster care agree that it might be the most viable solution. A new face of the child welfare system is that of fourteen-year-old Naika Venant. After bouncing in and out of state care, and from one foster home to another for ten years, on January 22, 2017, Naika hanged herself in her foster home's bathroom while live-streaming the event on Facebook.

However, the proponents of foster care aggressively defend the system. They say there is no going back to the misery and heartbreak that one could find on the pages of some Victorian novels. The sheer number of foster homes in the United States dictates the brutal statistical reality that some of them will be bad. If a phenomenon, no matter how horrible, exists in the entire American population, it will also be present in a cross-section of the population that represents foster care. Regardless of the occasional horrors, foster care is still the best option for children removed from homes, and it is as close to a family as some kids can get.

On the other hand, not all allegations of atrocities committed by foster parents are true. It is easy for a foster parent to accuse their foster children of lying, stealing, or committing some other petty crime. It is equally easy for foster children to accuse a foster parent of abuse. In the meantime, everyone agrees that although it is the best we have to offer, the system of foster care remains a bureaucratic nightmare.

CHAPTER EIGHTEEN

Foster Disaster

Most foster parents are good people who would never intentionally harm a child. They decide to foster because they found it morally compelling, or because they could not have children of their own but are not ready to adopt, or because they have something to share.

Many people who have already experienced fostering children have a message to those who are considering doing it: DON'T! According to data published on the Adoption in Child Time website, out of the estimated two-hundred thousand foster homes in the United States, thirty to fifty percent drop out each year. The turnover rate is even higher than in the fast-food industry, where people come and go all the time.

If you want to foster a child, first you have to go through what one foster parent described as a *bureaucratic anal probe*. Be prepared for a ton of personal questions.

Some will be very personal, like "Are you sexually active?" "Are you happy with your sex life?" You will be treated like a potential child molester, a potential psychopath, and a potential sadist. You will be asked about your finances and your spending habits. You will be viewed as a person trying to commit fraud against the state. If you want to be licensed, you will have to endure all of this with a smile on your face.

Then, you have to attend mandatory training, two to four hours on Saturday mornings or weekday evenings, for several months. You have to participate in each session, regardless of your professional background. A child psychologist with twenty years of experience must still attend the session, *ABC of Child Psychology*. A special education university professor must go to a session in which she will be taught the basics of special education. Since the system is a bureaucratic nightmare, everything must be done by the book.

You have to endure a thorough inspection of your house, during which you are expected to answer questions like, "Why do you keep your kitchen knives in the kitchen?" And answers like, "Because it is uncomfortable to cut a steak with a spoon" will not be appreciated. A bureaucrat with a sense of humor is an oxymoron. You will also have to draw a fire escape route, showing how a person will escape from the second story bedroom in case your house is on fire. In the future, you will be required to conduct fire drills with members of your household, although they may exclude your cat.

Finally, if you are lucky and live close enough to a private child welfare agency, a foster child will be placed in your house. From now on, you will be expected to manage kids who come from environments that are completely devoid of structure. Your foster children will turn your life into unimaginable chaos. They will provide you with a permanent headache. They will scream, bite, and kick you. They will punch you in the face. They will lie to you daily. They will be in constant trouble at school. They may torture your pets and go after your biological child, especially when you are not around. They will steal. They will cut themselves, run away, kill your big screen TV with a BB gun, or do something equally creative. They have no intention of hurting you physically or financially, but they just do not know any better. They almost unanimously have deep psychological wounds.

What about being a single foster parent? Most people might say that whoever takes this challenge must be a certifiable nut case and should see a mental health professional without delay. Yet, these people do exist. They are the unsung heroes, and they are accomplishing things that most of us would deem impossible.

A divorced woman, who just received her foster parent's license and was waiting for the first foster child to be placed with her, wrote on social media, "I am going to run a tight ship!" After having the fifth foster child placed in her house, the same woman wrote, "The ship is on fire!"

As stated before, foster parents face a multitude of challenges, but single foster mothers must face them alone. Frequently, they receive little or no support from their relatives, especially when they are planning to adopt a foster child. A common approach is, "Don't you have enough problems with your own kids?" The answer is, "Yes." Single mothers certainly have enough problems with their biological children, whom they also must handle alone. However, this may be the reason why they apply for a foster license. They think that between child support and a state-supplied stipend, perhaps they will be able to stay home, spend time with their biological children, and take care of the other children that are placed with them. Everyone will benefit, and everyone will be happy. There are also single women – and some-times men – who never marry and don't have a biological child. They believe that they have the emotional capacity to foster and maybe change a child's life. Until that ship catches fire; until there is no peaceful moment in that foster parent's life. But by that time, it is too late to go back.

A brand-new foster mom wrote on social media, "Y'all! This new mom life has me feeling like I'm losing my mind... halfway through our first 'road trip,' I had to check to see if I had a bra on or not! My life has been consumed by my little foster son! I had everything packed for him, and I barely packed anything for myself. My house is a disaster. When he goes to bed, I don't have the energy to do housework or eat. I just make sure I bathe myself and go to sleep because I know he is going to wake up multiple times in the night, and I have to be on my A-game at work. My days were off last week....

all day Friday, I thought it was Thursday. It's got to get easier, right?"

No, it doesn't get easier because parenting, by definition, is hard, and parenting children who were abused, neglected, or both, is an enormous challenge. Another single foster mom responded to that post with a joke:

"Me: I want a unicorn for Christmas."

"Santa: Please, be realistic."

"Me: OK, in that case, I want five minutes to myself each day to drink my coffee hot and to pee in peace."

"Santa: What color unicorn would you like?"

As a foster parent, you have to make sure your foster children take their meds. Oh yes, they will be heavily medicated whether you like it or not because, as described in another chapter of this book, the system believes that medicating is better than educating. At the end of a long day, you will be required to fill out a medication log. Since fostering a child is tied to a bureaucracy, and because bureaucracies love paperwork, a medication log will be just one of many mandatory forms: you may be required to keep a weekly activity log, in which you must list all spiritual activities, culturally enriching activities, social equality activities, intellectual activities, health-oriented activities, and whatever other activities crosses the mind of an ambitious bureaucrat. You will be wondering if a church picnic with a few rounds of Frisbee, attended by the only African American family in your community, and with hot dogs accompanied by a fresh pickle on the side can be considered spiritual, culturally enriching, socially equitable, intellectual, and health-oriented at the same time.

You are also required to be in touch with your foster child's agency, but do not expect them to do anything for you or for your foster kid. It is best to do exactly as told and never ask for anything. Your foster child's caseworker may have up to forty kids on her caseload. She is over-worked and probably underpaid. She lives in a state of constant stress, and she most likely questions her career choice every day.

You are also not permitted to cross state lines with your foster child unless you have submitted a formal written request, and it has been approved. Since fostering is state business, it must be conducted within the physical boundaries of the state. Taking a foster child to Disney World may be possible, but only if you are prepared to fight spectacular wars with an army of bureaucrats.

Do not form emotional bonds with your foster child. For most foster children, as stated before, the goal is reunification with their biological family, which means that the kid will not stay with you forever. The fact that you can provide much more than the child's biological mother is irrelevant. Fostering is temporary, and by the time you are really attached to a child, you will be saying goodbye.

You must also deal with your foster children's home visits, where their biological mother may tell them that they are stupid, ugly, and that they should never have been born. You must deal with a therapist, who should provide you with support and wisdom, but who is frequently underpaid, overworked, and unprepared for his roles. To give you an example, a single foster parent reported to her therapist that her nine-year-old foster daughter was scared to go on home visits to see her biological mom. The therapist responded, "I'm sure she is scared, and we don't want to discount her fear, but we have to remember she's gotten used to living in your secure, loving, safe home, and she's going to have time to get used to not having that."

Above all, you have to manage an unmanageable child. Your foster child may lie, steal, trash your house, scream, and yell. The child may use vulgarities and call you names. If a child was sexually abused, he or she might try to engage other children living under your roof in sexual activities, regardless of their age.

If you discipline a child in an attempt to put structure into his world of chaos, the child will retaliate by accusing you of abuse. The child will probably say that he or she has been sexually abused under your roof. Caseworkers are so attuned to this issue that they always ask the kids whether they have been molested. A foster child learns that making this accusation is a quick ticket out of a foster home that he or she does not like. In this case, a parent will not only lose the foster child, but no other foster children will be placed in his or her house. A foster parent will be stigmatized and penalized without a due process. Screaming, "But I have not done anything wrong!" will not help. The phenomenon is so widespread that a group of foster parents felt the need to create a National Foster Parent Coalition for Allegation Reform.

Because of the prevalence of real cases of sexual exploitation of foster children, caseworkers are excessively suspicious. They may interpret naturally occurring events as a prelude to something sinister and repulsive. In one real incident, a caseworker came into a foster home and saw a six-year-old foster child, a boy, sitting on the laps of his foster father, who was reading him a book. That foster father and his wife developed a strong emotional attachment with the boy, who has been with them since he was little more than a baby, and whom they were planning to adopt. In the minds of most people, an idyllic picture of a parent reading to a small child who sits on that parent's lap symbolizes a bond between parents and children. However, the caseworker did not see it that way. The caseworker saw physical contact, which in her eyes was inappropriate. She immediately removed the kicking and screaming child from a house where he was truly and deeply loved.

In general, it is recommended not to touch foster children placed under your care. There should be no hugs or kisses. Anthropologists may have published volumes on the positive effects of primates touching other primates. Psychologists may have added their own volumes on children's need to be hugged. However, in the bizarre world of foster care, touching children is taboo.

On top of all that, the foster care system usually experiences nothing but negative publicity. The media has no access to foster children until something horrible happens. When something does happen, it is considered an excellent human-interest story because it evokes anger and sympathy. The case receives a lot of publicity and creates an impression that all foster parents are monsters.

No wonder that after a year or two, most foster parents burn out. They find a different outlet for their unfulfilled compassion, go on a new crusade, and instead of hugging children, start hugging trees.

CHAPTER NINETEEN

Fostering Overseas

With so many problems nagging the foster care system in the United States, it may be worth checking if other countries handle things differently.

Our northern neighbor, Canada, has only about fifty thousand children in foster care, which is almost ten times less than the United States. However, Canada's population is thirty-five million, compared to three-hundred-twenty million in the US. Yet, Canada must be doing something right, because the majority of foster kids in Canada stay in care for less than six months. Additionally, over fifty percent are reunited with their biological families and never enter the system again.

There are approximately one million foster children in Europe. However, Europe has tied itself in a Gordian knot of young refugees who came mostly from Syria and who are in desperate need of assistance. In 2015, almost four hundred thousand asylum seekers in Europe were children, and one hundred thousand of them were unaccompanied minors. Based on the United Nations Convention on the Rights of the Child, they have "the right to enjoy the highest attainable standard of health." This means that children must receive all the kinds of assistance and support that the host countries are able to provide. "The right to enjoy the highest attainable standard of health" does not include keeping children in cages after they are forcibly separated from their parents, but that is an entirely different story.

In Europe, a lot of time and resources in child protective services currently focus on young refugees from Syria. One grueling repercussion of this recent exodus is underage brides. How do you treat a thirteen-year-old girl who has entered your country with her fifty-year-old husband? Should she be viewed as a spouse, or as a child victim of sexual exploitation? Should her husband be arrested and prosecuted as a pedophile? With lots of effort and open-mindedness, sixteen- to eighteen-year-old brides can be tolerated, but anyone younger than sixteen creates a legal and ethical nightmare. In some cases, young girls were removed from their much older husbands and placed in protective custody. Denmark even tried to put a ban on underage wives, and in consequence, two girls separated from their much older husbands attempted suicide.

Some people in the UK complain that many Middle-eastern men take advantage of the fact that they look young for their age, which helps them to more easily enter the country without documentation. Since assistance for underage refugees is more generous than what is offered to grownups, men who are in their late twenties claim that they are sixteen or seventeen and consequently are treated as kids.

Refugees aside, different countries in Europe have developed different approaches to foster care. Traditionally, in Mediterranean countries, like Italy or Spain, foster care is based on kinship. This is less prevalent in Great Britain or in Scandinavia, where most foster parents are typically not related to their foster kids.

Percentages of children in foster care also vary between countries. For example, in Latvia, 2.2 percent of all residents below the age of eighteen are in the care of the state, while in Sweden, that fraction represents just 0.66 percent. Although poverty should never be the only reason for removing a child from a home, it is nevertheless a universal truth that poverty breeds child abuse and neglect, so it should be noted that Latvia has more poverty than Sweden.

Alternatively, some countries in Europe have legal limitations that determine the maximum number of children allowed in a foster home. In Croatia, a foster couple can have only three foster children placed with them unless there is a larger group of siblings. A single foster parent can get no more than two foster kids, or just one if a child has a disability. In Finland, the maximum number of children per foster family is four, including foster parents' biological kids. These limitations have successfully eliminated the phenomenon of turning foster care into a moneymaking endeavor, which is an inarguable problem in the United States.

In the United States, foster parents are invariably required to go through training. However, in many European countries, it is not mandatory for the child's relatives. Europe has a legal ban on placing newborns and toddlers below the age of three in group homes or institutions. In a way similar to the system that is in place in the United States, older children are divided between foster homes and group homes. However, proportions between the two differ from one country to another. Ireland, Norway, Great Britain, and Sweden depend mostly on foster homes, while Germany, France, the Netherlands, and Hungry tend to place more children in group homes.

In all of Europe, foster care relies heavily on pedagogy, a social science that combines the theory and practice of teaching and caring for children. In Europe, pedagogy is a well-developed academic discipline studying different ways to nurture the development of a human being. While teachers focus on instruction, pedagogues are involved in the knowledge that will prepare children for adult life, such as social skills and cultural norms. In the EU, all employees of group homes and residential facilities for foster kids must have at least some degree of knowledge of pedagogy. Multidisciplinary teams that include social workers, psychologists, pedagogues, and teachers are all involved in making significant decisions regarding a foster child.

European countries agree that there is an urgent need for more studies regarding foster care outcomes. Some studies report that people who leave foster care suffer a heightened risk of being homeless, committing crimes, and having children at a young age, which mimics the studies done in the United States. The only exception is Finland, where a study of people between the ages of twenty-two and fifty-one, who used to be in foster care, shows that they are not different from the rest of society.

The current focus of foster care in Europe is involved in the overall development of children, and is not limited to responding to their immediate needs. There is a push to involve older children in foster care in the decision-making processes and making them take at least some responsibility for their choices, which is considered a significant step in the transition to adulthood.

Australia is still recovering from the shock caused by the phenomenon known as the Forgotten Australians. Between the end of the nineteenth century and 1970, as many as 150,000 British children were sent to overseas colonies, mostly Australia, New Zealand, South Africa, and sometimes Canada. Some of these children were as young as three. Consequently, the children were removed not only from their homes but also from their native country. Most were not orphans, but this was considered irrelevant. The decision to send these children abroad was usually made because it was cheaper to care for children in need in the Commonwealth countries than in Great Britain.

The Forgotten Australians also included Aboriginal children forcibly removed from homes, which was a practice similar to removing Native American kids from their parents and their tribal lands in the United States. The overall number of Forgotten Australians was estimated at half a million. Many were severely abused, neglected, and used as free labor.

Today, Australia has a system of foster care similar to that in the United States. In most cases, children removed from biological parents are in home-based care. Respite care provides short-term accommodations for children whose parents are unable to care for them temporarily. Like in the US, states and territories oversee the system, with limited involvement by the national government.

A transplant from Europe who married an American and now lives and works in the United States made an interesting remark. She said that in terms of work ethic and the approach to the workforce, the United States is halfway between Western Europe and Japan. The European Union mandates that all member states must, by law, grant their employees a minimum of four weeks of paid vacation per year. Germany, France, Italy, Spain, and the brexiting UK have most full-time employees working less than forty hours per week. In Western Europe, new parents enjoy more than one hundred days of paid family leave. On the other end of the spectrum, in Japan, many employees become enslaved by their companies. In recent years, Japan has been dealing with the epidemic of "karoshi," or suicides resulting from being overworked. The United States is somewhere in the middle of these two extremes.

The same may be true about the country's foster care system. Kanae Doi, a director of a Human Rights Watch in Japan, was quoted by newspapers saying, "It's heart-breaking to see children crammed into institutions and deprived of the chance for life in a caring family setting. While other developed countries place most vulnerable children in family-based care, in Japan, a shocking 90 percent end up in institutions." No wonder that one Japanese teenager and a recipient of the institutionalized care said, "I do not have dreams."

In terms of caring for orphaned or abused children, the United States is also in the middle. The US, with our very different political system, cannot be compared to Finland - a haven of socialist benefits provided by the government to the society. That said, some ideas, such as limiting the number of foster children placed in specific home, or involving pedagogy and some degree of self-determination in the process of caring for a foster child, may be worth a closer look. It would cost money and might require sacrifices, such as removing a tank or two from our ever-expanding defense budget, but if we do not care about protecting our children, who are we so eager to protect?

CHAPTER TWENTY

Little Hawk, Also Known as Mikey

While the Land Down Under is still dealing with the Forgotten Australians, the US must reconcile the dark pages of our own history. One of those dark pages deals with the forcible removal of Native American children and placing them in white boarding schools, or with white foster families.

The military campaigns against American Indians were expensive and unsuccessful. Despite killing them with weapons and diseases, by the end of the 19th century, the American Indians still stood proudly. This is when Brigadier Gen. Richard H. Pratt came up with a new idea. Rather than murdering Native Americans, it would be more efficient to destroy their culture, which was accomplished by removing Native American children from their families and their land and subjecting them to intense and extreme acculturation.

The first boarding school for Native American children, Carlisle Indian Industrial School, was opened in Pennsylvania in 1879, and was soon followed by others. They all operated with the blessing of the federal government. While the exact number of Native American children forcibly removed from homes is unknown, the number is estimated at hundreds of thousands. In 1925 alone, about 70,000 Native American kids, some as young as three, were placed in white boarding schools. That number represented eighty percent of all Native American children.

Upon entering a boarding school, Native kids were subjected to brutal assimilation with the dominant European culture. They had to assume new, European names. They had to speak only English – their native languages were strictly forbidden, and so were their ancestral religious beliefs and customs. They all had to become "good Christians." The boys also had to follow the "haircut order." Wearing the long hair that was traditional to their culture was forbidden.

White America used Native American kids to conduct a systemic cultural genocide on the native residents of this land. Many Native American parents did not even know what happened to their children or where they were placed. Even more horribly, this practice is continued today in immigrant detention centers for kids along the southern border of the United States.

The white boarding schools for Native American children were overcrowded, poorly funded, and had deplorable living conditions. The kids were routinely malnourished. Many died from diseases, such as tuberculosis, or the flu. Many children just vanished, and their parents never knew what happened to their offspring. Nobody seemed to care.

Finally, in 1978, the US Congress adopted an Indian Child Welfare Act, which put an end to the practice of the forcible removal of Native American kids from their homes. Among other things, this act requires that when a Native American child is orphaned or removed from biological parents who are deemed unfit to take care of the kid, tribal authorities should be involved in the decision of what happens to the child. First consideration is given to the extended family members willing to foster or adopt. If no relatives can be located, the child should be placed with an unrelated tribal family. Finally, if no family can be found, tribal elders may reach out to another tribe to find an appropriate placement.

Does this mean that another dark page in US history was finally put to rest? Not really. The issue resurfaced in 2019 and is creating a brand-new legal nightmare. In Texas, a white couple adopted a 3-year-old Native American boy named Zachary. The boy's biological mom was Navajo, and his father was Cherokee. At first, the Navajo Nation brought objections to the adoption of Zachary, which violated the Indian Child Welfare Act. However, after giving consideration to the fact that the boy spent almost one-and-a-half years with his white family and was already attached to his new parents, the Navajo Nation withdrew their objections.

This would have been the end of the case if not for Zachary's Navajo mother, who gave birth to another child, this time a girl. Due to a long history of drug problems, the Navajo mom was still unfit to be a parent, and the newborn girl had to be removed. Zachary's white parents immediately petitioned for her adoption, claiming that the siblings should grow up together. The Navajo Nation again refuted this. They located a relative, a traditional Native American woman and a relative, able and willing to take care of the girl.

Once again, the case went to court, and the Texas judge ruled that the Navajo baby-girl should be placed with the couple that adopted her older brother. The parents pointed out that they could provide much better living conditions for the girl. The mom works as a physician, and the dad is a civil engineer. They are both devout Christians.

While announcing his ruling, the judge also said that the Indian Child Welfare Act of 1978 was unconstitutional because it gave preference based on race. The entire population of federally recognized Native Americans collectively gasped, and the case started a long journey through multiple levels of American jurisprudence. This case is still ongoing, and will probably end up in the Supreme Court.

Should race be a factor when a child is placed in a foster home? Perhaps African American foster children should only be placed with African American foster parents. Maybe Hispanic foster kids should go to the Hispanic homes, and white kids should be with white families. Only there is no such thing as a Hispanic race, and there is definitely no separate race for Native Americans. Anyone who has ever attended a large pow-wow must have noticed that there are American Indians with blond hair and blue eyes. There are also American Indians who are black. Being a Native American is about culture, language, and tradition, and not about race.

Zachary's white parents can probably provide his little sister with more material possessions. She will have her own room, maybe her own big-screen TV, video games, designer clothes, and a beautiful back yard. But she will not stand on the hills of her native land, a free-range expanding forever in each direction, and she will not hear the voices of her ancestors carried in the wind, whispering to her in their native tongue.

What do we value more, our heritage, or our bank accounts?

The Supreme Court will have a difficult decision to make. Perhaps to seek wisdom, the judges should visit the cemetery of Native American children who died in Carlisle Indian Industrial School. They are still there – rows of white gravestones, far away from their land and their people. In 2017, Northern Arapahos successfully petitioned the US government to return the remains of two boys to their native land in Wyoming, but the rest of the children were left behind. Apache, Sioux, Cheyenne, Nez Perce, Oneida, Comanche, Cherokee, Seneca, Eskimo, Chippewa, Crow, Paiute, Shoshone, and the list goes on... All died alone, far away from their homes. All died as Native Americans, before being appropriately "assimilated."

CHAPTER TWENTY-ONE

The Wolves and the Lambs

In January 2010, the residents of Manhattan's Lower East Side were treated to a scene that was bizarre even by New York standards. An individual, who seemed to be a young male with unusually long hair, aimlessly walked the streets wearing a Mike Meyers mask. Finally, somebody called the cops. The officers tried to interview the young man, but he did not speak. They took him to Bellevue and kept him there for a week, but after that, he was permitted to go home.

Soon after the incident, the story exploded and culminated in a critically acclaimed documentary, *The Wolfpack*. But the horrifying Angulo family saga started long before that, in South America, on a picturesque trail leading to Machu Picchu. This is where, in 1989, an adventurous free spirit from Indiana named Susanne Reisenbichler met a Peruvian man named Oscar Angula.

He was a follower of Hare Krishna and, by all reports, had quite a few unorthodox views. They married and moved to the United States.

Upon arriving in the US, Oscar was not interested in pursuing gainful employment. Instead, he planned to become a rock star. While busy with seeking stardom, he allowed his rapidly growing family to live mostly in a van. Finally, in 1996, the Angulos moved to a housing project on Manhattan's East Side. At that time, Oscar and Susanne had five kids, including a girl with Turner Syndrome, and four boys. Two of them were twins. Two more boys were born in New York. All children had names borrowed from Sanskrit: Vishnu, Govinda, Narayana, Mukunda, Bhagavan, Krisna, and Jagadisa. The boys were not allowed to cut their hair because, according to their dad, long hair was a source of strength.

Oscar Angulo imprisoned his wife and children in the New York apartment for fourteen years. He had the only key to the apartment, and he would also block the front door with a ladder. Sometimes, his wife and kids were allowed to take brief, supervised walks outside once or twice a year, but there were also years when they never left. The apartment, located on the 16th floor of the building, had six rooms, but two were off-limits to the kids because they shared the walls with neighbors. Oscar did not want anyone to know about his prisoners.

The family lived like some strange, isolated tribe, away from everything and everyone. Oscar told the kids that the world outside was dangerous, evil, and that they must never interact with strangers. During their rare and brief walks, they weren't even allowed to make eye contacts with strangers. To Susanne's relatives, back in the Midwest, she vanished without a trace.

Susanne, who once hiked in the Himalayas, was now her husband's strangely compliant prisoner, with even more rules to obey than the kids. However, she remained a loving mother. She homeschooled the children, teaching them about the world outside of their Lower East Side apartment, and encouraged their creativity. The family lived off of welfare and Susanne's meager homeschooling income.

The boys were allowed two forms of entertainment: music and movies. The movies soon became their love and obsession. They later claimed that they watched over ten thousand films, many multiple times. They created painstakingly handwritten scripts that they learned by heart, and recreated entire scenes. Using only paper, scissors, glue, cereal boxes, and other everyday objects, they made terrific costumes. To the Angulo boys, movies carried the full power of their imagination. From time to time, they would look out of the windows and at the strange world outside that, in their minds, was less real than the movies they watched.

In 2009, Oscar covered the apartment's windows with blankets. From now on, nothing from the outside world, not even sunlight, was allowed into his domain. Maybe the act of blocking the sunlight, or perhaps the boys' age and growing curiosity was the spark that ignited the rebellion. In January 2010, while his father went shopping for groceries, fifteen-year-old Mukunda gathered all of his courage, hid his face behind a Mike Meyers mask, and wandered outside into the unknown world of Manhattan.

Although Mukunda ended up in Bellevue and did not dare to speak to anyone, his brave act led to a full-blown mutiny. The other Angulo brothers soon followed Mukunda, and eventually, the world learned about their existence. By pure coincidence, one of the first outsiders they met and befriended was a filmmaker, Crystal Moselle. She decided to approach this strange looking pack of longhaired boys who wore sunglasses and dressed like characters from *The Reservoir Dogs*. Crystal directed a documentary about the Angulo family, *The Wolfpack*. Upon its release, the entire world met the Angulo boys and found out that they were charming, intelligent, polite, and amazingly creative. The world watched them start brand new adventures, like feeling sand underneath their feet, running through an orchard, or touching the water of the Atlantic. The world also met their mother, Susanne, who followed her sons in reclaiming freedom and independence from her paranoid and mentally unstable husband.

Today, the Angulo brothers live normal lives, and only a couple of them maintain a superficial relationship with their father. Susanne is estranged from her husband and even changed her last name back to Reisenbichler. However, she continued homeschooling her youngest son, and she still takes care of her disabled daughter. *The Wolfpack* story seems to have a happy ending, but people are still asking questions and in an attempt to understand how such a thing could happen in the first place. How can individuals be locked away, unnoticed, unseen, and unmissed by society for fourteen years, inside a building with over eight hundred residents? How is it possible that Child Protective Services never knew and never got involved? How could Susanne remain passive for all those years? Was she really another victim, or a willing participant? Why didn't she break free sooner, instead of staying with her weird husband and even trying to justify his abuse after their story was made public?

January must be the get-out-of-jail month for children imprisoned by their parents. In January 2018, almost exactly eight years after Mukunda's escape, Riverside County Sheriff's Department in California responded to a 9-1-1 call made by a teenage girl. The girl said, "I live in a family of fifteen. (My mother) doesn't take care of us. They only chain us up if we do something wrong. My sisters, they wake up at night, and they will start crying, and they wanted me to call somebody…I wanted to call y'all, so y'all can help my sister."

When deputies entered the house, they encountered a scene from a nightmare. The place was dark and foul smelling that it was hard to breathe. There were piles of trash everywhere, mixed with human feces covering the floors. A frail-looking young man was shackled to the bed with a chain and a padlock. At the same time, two adults, apparently the parents, were in the process of unchaining two younger kids. There were thirteen children in the house, and their age ranged between two to twenty-nine. However, this could only be established later because, except for the toddler, all the children looked much younger than their age. The boy still chained to the bed was twenty-two. He spent six-and-a-half years of his young life being restrained, first with ropes and later with chains. The oldest one, a twenty-nine-year-old woman, weighed only 82 pounds. The brave girl who escaped and called the authorities was seventeen, but she was so small and thin that, at first, the deputies assumed she was ten.

The girl planned her escape for two years. She climbed out of the window with one of her sisters, but the other girl was too scared and went back. The seventeen-year-old used a deactivated cell phone she found inside the house and managed to hide. This is how the world found out about the Turpin Suburban House of Horrors.

This story starts in West Virginia, where, in 1985, a local girl named Louise married a promising young engineer, David Turpin. Louise was just sixteen, eight years younger than her husband. They were both Pentecostals and strong supporters of the Quiverfull movement, which teaches that all children are gifts from God, encouraging procreation and prohibiting contraceptives. At some point, Louise Turpin said that she would like to have twenty children.

The young couple moved to Texas, where they bought a property in Rio Vista and later in Fort Worth. David worked as an engineer for Lockheed Martin and Northrop Grumman and, at some point, earned a salary of $140,000 per year. In Texas, Louise diligently gave birth to their first child. Then another, and another, and another… She never stopped.

The neighbors eventually noticed that something was not quite right with that rapidly growing family. A neighbor recollected that one day, she encountered one of the Turpin children and was surprised to see that the shabby-dressed girl was wearing gloves. Her surprise turned into shock when she realized that there were no gloves; the girl's hands were clean while her arms and the rest of her body were covered with a thick layer of dirt. The girl explained that washing hands above the wrists wasted water. When asked about her name, the girl responded that they were not allowed to tell their names to strangers.

One of the Turpin girls, probably the oldest, even attended a local school for a while. She always wore rags, and she smelled so bad that she was mercilessly teased and bullied by other kids. But one day, all of the Turpin kids disappeared. On rare occasions, one or two would be seen from a distance, but they no longer interacted with neighbors, nor were they allowed to have contact with other kids. In Texas, even more than in other states, people follow the *mind-your-own-business* approach. Nobody cared what was going on behind the walls of the Turpin's place, and nobody suspected that the house might hide dirty secrets. Child Protective Services were never called and were never involved. The authorities were called to the Turpin residence twice, but only because of a dog attack and a missing pig.

And then, out of the blue, the entire Turpin family was gone. They moved out. Afterward, some of the neighbors entered the abandoned house for the first time. They will never forget what they saw.

Again, the first thing that hit them was the overpowering stench. The carpet was ripped up, and somebody covered the subfloor with plywood, which was dirty and full of holes and stains. There was trash everywhere, in some places up to the waist. All the walls were smeared with human feces. The neighbors found several dead dogs and cats. There were scratch marks on the doors, and at first, the neighbors assumed the animals made them. However, after the Turpin story broke out, they were no longer so sure. It was also strange that somebody made vents inside the closets – probably because the kids were locked there. There were padlocks on everything: the bathroom door, the refrigerator, the cabinets, and even the toy boxes. There were rows of bunk beds in one room, which looked like dirty and neglected military barracks. Ropes hung from the beds. One of the women later recollected that she thought it would be unsafe to allow kids to play with a rope in a bunkbed. It never crossed her mind that the rope was used to tie the kids to the beds. For the lack of a better word, the place was described as being in total and complete squalor. Yet, nobody notified the authorities.

In the meantime, despite David's significant income, the Turpins filed for bankruptcy. Their insanity was evolving. Back in Texas, the mom and dad moved from neglect to neglect and abuse of their children. In sunny California, they progressed from neglect and abuse, to unimaginable physical and mental torment. Since one of the boys, probably the oldest, learned how to escape the ropes, the Turpins replaced them with chains. From now on, the kids were chained to beds for weeks, sometimes even for months. Trips to the bathroom were not allowed. The children slept during the day and were awake at night to avoid detection. They were punished for even the smallest disobedience. They were fed only once a day, although the mom and dad would put pies on the countertops. Their starving children were allowed to look but not to eat. The house was full of toys – mostly still in their original boxes and wrappings. The kids were not allowed to play with them, and they had no access to television or any real schooling. The only activity that was permitted was writing in their journals. Each child was allowed one shower per year.

Surprisingly, from time to time, the family made long trips to Disneyland, the Grand Canyon, or Las Vegas. The Turpins would later post pictures of their children, usually wearing the same clothes, exceptionally thin but smiling. By all appearances, they were images of a big and happy family. At the time of her arrest, Louise gave birth to thirteen kids and planned at least one more.

Until one night, in January of 2018, seventeen-year-old Jordan Turpin made her brave escape. The authorities entered the house on a beautiful, middle-class subdivision in Perris, California, and finally freed the tortured kids. All the children were taken to a hospital, while the mom and dad went straight to jail.

The children were exposed to inhumane treatment for so long that they "lacked the basic knowledge of life."

Years had passed since any one of them had seen a doctor, and none of them ever went to a dentist. They did not know the meaning of such words as police, medication, or pills. They were beaten, shackled, kept in restrains, and sometimes strangled. They were victims of systemic and calculated torture. At least one girl was sexually abused by her father. Except for the toddler, they were all severely malnourished, in fact, emaciated, which resulted in cognitive issues and nerve damage. Two of the Turpin daughters are now unable to bear children.

The trial of David and Louise Turpin ended in April 2019. They both pleaded guilty to fourteen counts of torture, adult abuse, child endangerment, false imprisonment, and the list goes on and on. They were sentenced to 25 years to life.

All the kids were discharged from a hospital. The older ones, young adults between the ages of eighteen and twenty-nine, currently live together in an undisclosed location. They are slowly learning about life. They pick citrus, make ice-cream sundaes, and cook Mexican food. They are very friendly and are purportedly doing great.

The younger kids are in foster care and in the process of being adopted. Supposedly, they will be adopted together. They are in touch with their older siblings. Due to the notoriety of the Turpin case, the people in charge are making sure that the privacy of the Turpin children is protected, and that their location is not disclosed.

While every single aspect of this case is, in the least, shocking, perhaps the biggest surprise came during Turpins' sentencing hearing, when some of their kids…

forgave them. Their son, identified as John Doe 2, said, "I love my parents and have forgiven them for a lot of the things they did to us." Another kid said, "I love both of my parents so much. Although it may not have been the best way of raising us, I am glad that they did because it made me the person I am today." A daughter suggested that their sentence must not be too harsh, and that twenty-five year is excessive. Yes, they have suffered, but she believed that their parents had good intentions and never really wanted to hurt anyone.

Both the Turpin and the Angulo children spent years imprisoned by their parents. They were both isolated and deprived of the opportunity to interact with the world outside. However, this is where the similarities end.

Oscar Angulo was paranoid with extreme controlling behaviors, which indicated a severe personality disorder, but he did not torture his children. He allowed them to have entertainment, although only within the confines of their Manhattan apartment. They might not have had access to delicacies, but they were provided with regular meals. Considering the circumstances, they received a reasonably decent education, and they were encouraged to develop their artistic spirit. Above all, they experienced love, definitely from their mother but also, in his own twisted way, from their father.

The unfathomable compliancy of the mother is difficult to explain. She definitely exhibited the non-combatant attitude of a person who avoids confrontation, but there was almost certainly more going on. Susanne may have suffered from Stockholm syndrome, a well-known phenomenon where hostages or other captives develop a bond or an alliance with their captors. We are all products of our environments. To all of us, the environment in which we live and to which we are exposed for an extended period of time is what we consider normal. To Susanne, her imprisonment became her reality, and she may have even rationalized the extreme limitations imposed by her husband. Within the confines of their prison, she tried to do the best she could for her kids.

The kids, both the Angulos and the Turpins, were also conditioned to their respective environments. They did not know the alternative because they never had an opportunity to experience it. Some people ask why none of the kids were sent to a regular school after being released. The older ones do take college classes, but for the younger kids, a regular school would be another nightmare. They would not know what to do, how to act, and how to behave. To them, everything would be new and unknown.

Many of them forgave their parents, partially due to the Stockholm syndrome, but also because of other reasons that are harder to explain. Children have such a strong need to be loved by parents that sometimes they conflate abuse with love.

The case of the Turpin parents was unique. Child abuse is, unfortunately, not uncommon, but being abused to this extreme and by both parents is rare. One reporter involved with the case asked a question about the Turpin parents that all of us would like to ask: "Are they certifiably nuts?" Knowing that David and Louise

Turpin were certifiably nuts would at least provide some explanation, but this was not the case. They knew exactly what they were doing, and they deliberately exposed their children to calculated, premeditated, and unusual torment. They were monsters, and they were sadists who apparently enjoyed imposing physical and psychological torture.

One question that relates to both stories, and also directly relates to theme of this book, is why were Child Protective Services never involved? The answer is sad yet undeniable. They were not engaged because they were never notified. This leads us to another, perhaps even more relevant question, why were they never told? This answer is more complicated. They were never notified because we live in a society that, like those neighbors in Texas, believes in minding one's own business. We Americans do not like to interfere with the private lives of our fellow Americans. We may have similar cultural roots as the Europeans, but unlike Europeans, we do not enjoy sharing our space. We are ready to fiercely defend it. Our homes are our castles.

A woman from Germany visited her American relatives who lived in the suburbs of a big city. The suburb looked more or less like the area the woman came from, not far from Munich. However, one conversation about the similarities of both places shocked the German. At one point, she asked, "You do not socialize with them? You have lived here for more than ten years, yet you don't even know their names? *Aber das ist unmöglich!*" No, despite what the woman from Germany might think, this is not only possible but it is also commonplace in the US. We are OK with the unorthodox, the unusual, even the weird because this is how we express our freedom. And most of the time, this approach works for us. However, there may be cases, like those mentioned above, when this privacy backfires.

It is hard to believe that Angulo's neighbors did not notice that there was a bunch of children living in that apartment on the 16th floor. Or maybe they did see, but thought that the family was fine. Some say that state school authorities should have known, but this isn't necessarily true – our laws allow for homeschooling. In most states, the procedure is relatively simple, and although some homeschooling parents abuse this right, most do not. This choice is another one of our freedoms, and we are not ready to give it up.

With all this said, one could also claim that Americans suffer from a Hero Complex. This is also who we are. We run to save the innocent, even if it might cause our own demise. Yet, the neighbors in Texas saw the deplorable conditions inside the Turpins' abandoned house. They knew that children lived there, but they did not call anyone. In California, one neighbor, who used to work late, saw a strange middle-of-the-night procession of children inside the Turpins place. He thought it was weird, yet did nothing.

To find an explanation, we must dig deep into the annals of social psychology, where one can find a phenomenon called bystander effect, or bystander apathy. Even when we notice something that should be reported, we know that other people see the same thing, and we assume that someone else will make the call. This happens frequently when, for example, people witness a car accident. A lot for cars can pass by, yet nobody calls 9-1-1 because everyone thinks that someone else must have already called. Ironically, the higher the number of bystanders, the less likely it is for someone to call for help.

If we could change this approach, a lot of children might be saved from abuse, sometimes even from death, and society is moving in the right direction. Social media is flooded with videos showing police misconduct toward minorities. Terrorist attacks have taught us another lesson. If you use public transportation, you hear frequent announcements about suspicious packages: *If you see something, say something.*

The same rule applies to children in distress: if you see or hear something, call the police or notify Child Protective Services in your state. An excellent 24-hour National Child Abuse Hotline is offered by an organization called Childhelp and supported by the U.S. Department of Health and Human Services. It can be accessed by calling or texting to (1-800) 4-A-CHILD or 1-800-422-4453.

The Childhelp website says, "An abuser's best friend is silence: the silent fear of the victim and the silence of those who could report." Regardless of whether you are a mandated reporter or just a citizen, and regardless of whether you subscribe to the *mind-your-own-business* approach, a simple call may save a child's life.

CHAPTER TWENTY-TWO

Foster Lullaby

A brief version of this story, by an anonymous author, appeared on social media in Central Europe. It was translated into English and adapted for this publication.

"Hello, is this Lost and Found?" asked a child's voice.

"Yes, it is, honey. Gabriel speaking. Did you lose something?"

"I lost my mom. Did you find her?"

"Can you give me a description?"

"Well, she is very good and very sweet and very beautiful. She has long black hair. Oh, and she loves cats and children."

"Let me see… Yesterday, we found one mom that matches this description. Maybe she is yours. Where are you calling from? Is it the Sunnybrook Residential Facility for foster children?"

"Yes, it is. Did she tell you she was my mom? Mommy! Mommy!!!" The boy was awakened by his own scream. He had the same dream night after night, and it always ended before he could be reunited with his lost mom. Something fell from his bed, and the boy gently picked it up from the floor. It was a picture of a young woman with long black hair holding a fat tabby cat. The boy found the picture on the street outside his group home and believed it was his mom. He kissed the picture and put it under his pillow. Like the previous night, and the night before, and the one before that, he cried himself to sleep.

The next morning, a director of the Sunnybrook Residential Facility found the picture under the boy's pillow. The director immediately recognized the young woman. She used to volunteer in the facility, and this is when she must have lost the photo. The young woman was trying to obtain a foster parent's license and later maybe adopt a child. But the process was painfully slow, and the director knew that the young woman's chances were limited. She was single, and the agency preferred placing foster children with married couples.

The director went back to her office, sat down, and waited. After a while, somebody knocked on the door, and the young woman from the picture stepped into the office.

"Here are my documents," she said, putting a thick folder on the director's desk. "Financial statements, house inspection results, well-water tests results, recommendations, verification of employment, background check…"

"Let me ask you something," interrupted the director. "Do you want a boy or a girl? Caucasian, African American, maybe Hispanic? Do you have a preference regarding the child's age? Would you like to look at pictures of our children?"

"I have no preferences, and I do not want to look at your pictures. I want to be a real mom. And real parents do not choose a child. They don't know if they are going to have a girl or a boy. They don't know if their child is going to be healthy or pretty or smart. Parents just love their children as they are. So please, give me the child who needs me the most."

"Hmmm… I have been doing this job for twenty-five years, and this is the first time a prospective foster parent has said something like this. I may have a child for you. It is a boy, five-years-old. His case is a very sad one. His mother was a junkie and overdosed soon after he was born. No father was listed on his birth certificate, and as far as we know, no father was ever in the picture. For years, the boy bounced from one relative to another, but he was never loved or wanted. And there were signs of physical abuse. Somebody used that child as a punching bag. He was brought to a hospital with a fractured arm, and they discovered old scars as well. This is how he ended up with us. Give me a moment."

The director left and returned a few minutes later with a little boy. When the child saw the young woman, his eyes grew big, and he threw himself at her with all his strength.

"Mom! Mommy! They've found you! I knew you were going to come for me! I knew it!"

The young woman held the little boy in her arms and asked with a trembling voice, "When can we start visitations? Is there a chance for an overnight stay before the Holidays?"

"The boy can go home with you today," said the director.

"But my paperwork, the medical records, the parenting classes…"

"Not required," interrupted the director. "We are running a special today. A child can go home with his new mom right away."

The young woman said quietly to the boy, "My house is small, but it will be perfect for us. And you are going to love the back yard. Especially my old oak tree in the corner, which is an excellent spot for a tree house, if someone could help us build one."

"Do you have a cat?" asked the little boy.

"I have two," the young woman's smile became even brighter. "Do you like cats?"

"Like them? They are my fa-vo-ri-test animals in the entire world!"

"Then, we will have to make a trip to an animal shelter because you are going to need your very own kitten," said the young woman.

The director watched them leave. The little boy held the young woman's hand the entire time, probably to make sure that he would not lose his mom again. The director smiled and dialed a number on her cell phone.

"Hello, Angels?"

"Yes, Gabriel here."

"This is Paula. I am reporting that the task is complete. The boy has been placed with his assigned mom."

"Good job, Paula. Have a nice day."

"Wait a minute, there are a few things we are going to need to make it work."

"What is it?"

"First of all, I want her paperwork done and approved by the end of the business day. And make sure that there is no red tape."

"You got it."

"Also, she needs more money. Nothing excessive or extravagant, but she must take care of a child. And little boys grow fast and have to eat well."

"Anything else?"

"Yes, she needs a good man. And don't interrupt me; I know there is a shortage, but she could use some help with the child. If possible, find her a carpenter."

"A carpenter?"

"Just do it. I will email you everything I have said so that you don't mess up again."

"Anything you say, Paula."

When the day was over, the little boy was tucked into bed. He was still holding the young woman's hand. She sat next to him and read him a story from a book, which her grandmother gave her when the young woman was a little girl. It was a story about an ugly duckling that grew up to be the most beautiful swan. The boy's eyes were closed, but a smile on his face indicated that he was still listening. A tabby cat, who would probably benefit from going on a diet, lay next to the boy's feet purring with delight. The cat was the only one who could see an angel gently kissing the little boy's forehead.

****

Whether or not you believe in angels, be an angel to a child in need.

THE END

If you enjoyed this book and found some benefit in reading it, I would like to hear from you and hope that you could take some time to post a review on Amazon. Your feedback and support will be appreciated.

Visit author's website at:
https://jcpater.com

Coming soon…

Rehomed

STORIES ABOUT ADOPTION

Please, turn this page for a preview

Kids with Return Receipts

There are no official statistics on failed international adoptions, but the number is high. Some sources suggest that it may be above twenty-five percent. The American public started realizing that there was a problem after an infamous case of a seven-year-old adoptee from Russia, Artyom Savelyev.

Artyom spent only about six months in the United States. After that, his adoptive mother, Torry-Ann Hansen, put little Artyom on a plane and sent him back to Russia. The boy was traveling alone with a *To-Whom-It-May-Concern* note from his new mom saying, "I no longer wish to parent this child. As he is a Russian national, I am returning him to your guardianship and would like the adoption disannulled." In Russia, nobody knew that Artyom was coming. Nothing was arranged for his return. Regardless, Ms. Hansen believed that her action was justified because the kid was "mentally unstable," "violent," and "not right in his mind." Therefore, in Ms. Hansen's eyes, putting a seven-year-old all alone on the plane and shipping him into nowhere, thousands of miles away, was entirely rational.

Several factors contribute to the frequent failures of international adoptions. While people adopting from the US foster system are required to go through parenting classes, there is little or no training available to parents adopting overseas. They often have unrealistic expectations based on stereotypes acquired from literature and movies. They do not know that adoptees, and especially older adoptees, are coming with baggage that needs to be handled with care. Even children adopted overseas as babies may have congenital issues that their adoptive parents should be aware of. For example, if you adopt from Russia or Ukraine, there is a high probability that a baby was born with fetal alcohol syndrome. If you adopt from Sub-Saharan Africa, you should be prepared that the child may be HIV positive.

Cultural and linguistic barriers are tough to overcome. We are all products of our environments and a child brought from South America, or Africa, or Asia comes with very different life experiences than a child born and raised in the United States, even if that American child has been in foster care. Kids adopted from foreign countries eat different foods, they laugh at different things, and they may have a system of norms and beliefs which their American adoptive parents are not familiar with and often cannot understand. A typical example is an African or Asian child who is avoiding eye-contact with grownups. It that child's culture, looking into the eyes of an older person or a person of authority, would be considered challenging and impolite. To the American adoptive parents, if the child cannot look you in the eyes, it is because the child lies or at least has something to hide. Consequently, children are judged and punished because they are misunderstood.

Some unwanted children adopted from other countries are warehoused in residential facilities, arranged through private insurance. Some are kicked out when they are sixteen or eighteen and have to fend for themselves, often joining the ranks of the American homeless. Another common practice is recycling adopted children and transferring them from one family to another.

In 2013, Reuters investigative journalists published an article, "The Child Exchange," subtitled, "Inside America's Underground Market for Adopted Children." The article explained how American adoptive parents, who no longer wanted children that they brought from a foreign country, were able to use the Internet to abandon the kids. It traced more than five thousand cases for five years. Adopted children, six to fourteen-year-old but sometimes as young as ten months, were being rehomed with new families. The process was usually simple and done with a power of attorney or guardianship. Although legally dubious, it was happening without much interference from the authorities. People were just handing over adopted children whom they no longer wanted to strangers without much consideration for the fact that some of those strangers might have been human traffickers, abusers, or pedophiles.

After the article was published, Yahoo shut down the rehoming sites claiming a violation of the company's terms-of-service. However, the practice continues, although now it is camouflaged under some forms of oversight. The Internet is still offering moving adoptees who are no longer wanted to new families through the process, which is usually mediated by private agencies for a substantial fee. It is no more ethical than handing over an unwanted child to a stranger, but it is more expensive. Adoptive parents convince themselves that since they are paying for this service, it must be alright.

As recently as in April 2018, investigative reporters from WKYC in Ohio came up with a story proving that rehoming or trafficking of children who were adopted from foreign countries, is not only very much alive but thriving. The story focused on Nita, brought to the United States from an orphanage in Haiti when she was thirteen. Her journey across the United States started in Idaho, but after a while, her American parents decided that it was not a good fit and sent Nita to Ohio, where she lived with a Christian family with thirty-three children. Nita stayed there for four months. After that, she was shipped to a different family in Idaho. From there, she was "rehomed" again, and once more sent to Ohio, to a family with nine kids. When Nita found out that some of them were molested by the father and brought it up to the attention of her new mother, she was immediately put on a plane back to Idaho, without even her purse. All of that rehoming and traveling back and forth between Idaho and Ohio happened within two years and after signing simple power of attorney forms that can be downloaded from the Internet. No courts, lawyers, or child welfare agencies were involved.

Ohio is one of just a handful of states that took steps to end this legal although dubious and unregulated practice of "rehoming" children. California is also trying to enact legislation to protect children from being moved from one adoptive family to another without legal oversight. However, at this point, "rehoming" is still alive and well. There are easily accessible websites offering children's galleries where one can look at pictures and pick a child. One search, for a Caucasian female, thirteen to seventeen-year-old, generated two hundred five results. A potential child molester or an aspiring serial killer can choose from blonds to red-haired, to brunettes, from petite to robust, all innocent and sweet. All unwanted. All ready to be disposed of, like trash.

Torture and Prayers

To Lydia Schatz, the town of Paradise, California, was hardly a paradise. It was more like hell. This is where Lydia died, tortured until she stopped breathing because she misspelled a word. Lydia was only seven-years-old. She was adopted by a Christian fundamentalist couple who believed in beating children in the name of Jesus. On the day she died, Lydia was beaten for seven hours with a quarter-inch plastic tubing, although there were short breaks for prayers. When paramedics came to the scene, Lydia was still alive, but she did not make it to the hospital. Her sister, eleven-year-old Zariah, also a victim of daily physical abuse, was critical after sustaining severe injuries but survived.

Kevin and Elizabeth Schatz adopted Lydia and two other children from Liberia. They already had six kids of their own. All the children were homeschooled. The Schatz followed the teachings of an evangelical preacher from Tennessee, Michael Pearl. Pearl published a book,

"To Train Up a Child," which became an instant success in the Christian fundamentalist circles and sold over one million copies. Among other things, the book is recommending beating a five-month-old on her bare legs, spanking a three-year-old "until he is totally broken," sitting on a child while administering corporal punishment, and if a child is still defiant, spanking him again. Preacher Pearl, the man of God, is explicitly recommending a quarter-inch plastic tubing for beating. He also provides advice that may apply to children who were adopted and, therefore, not trained through abuse since infancy: "If you are just beginning to institute training on an already rebellious child (…) then use whatever force is necessary to bring him to bay." Little Lydia must have been *already rebellious* because her adoptive parents used whatever force was necessary to bring her to a bay. They were both found guilty and are currently serving long prison terms.

About one year later, Hana, a thirteen-year-old adoptee from Ethiopia, died a horrible death in rural Washington state, sixty miles north of Seattle. Hana's adoptive parents, Carri and Larry Williams were blessed with only seven biological children, which is why they felt that they had to adopt more. They selected Hana and her deaf younger brother, Immanuel. The Williamses, also fundamentalist Christians, believed that children should live pious lives and not have access to TV or the Internet. All of their kids were homeschooled, and the family lived in total isolation. Perhaps not surprisingly, some of Ms. Williams' views were strikingly similar to the Islamic Sharia law. For example, according to Ms. Williams, women should not wear swimsuits or vote.

The Williamses also followed the child-rearing techniques recommended by preacher Pearl in his best-seller "To Train Up a Child." Hana was considered rebellious. Because of that, she often slept in a barn or was locked in a closet. She had to use an outhouse, and she showered outside with a garden hose. She was frequently refused shoes and clothes other than a towel. Her head was shaved. She had to eat leftovers and food that was still frozen. She was given sandwiches deliberately soaked in water. She was regularly punished and spanked with a variety of objects.

On a fatal night, in the spring of 2011, Hana was serving another of her punishments. She had to stand outside for hours - in the rain and near-freezing temperatures - wearing only sweat pants and a short-sleeved shirt. She fell several times. The family was watching from the inside of the house as Hana took off her clothes and started trashing.

People suffering from extreme hypothermia are known to undress in what is called a *hypothermic paradoxical disrobing*. They are hallucinating, and because at this point their nerves are severely damaged, they feel irrationally hot. In the last attempt to survive, the body is trying to warm up only the most essential internal organs. Cases of *hypothermic paradoxical disrobing* were observed on multiple occasions in the extreme environment of Mount Everest's Death Zone. However, Hana's adoptive mother viewed her undressing as indecent and therefore deserving even more punishment. Not far from the headquarters of Microsoft, Starbucks, and Expedia, a beautiful little girl with a captivating smile, slowly died of hypothermia and malnutrition.

When Ms. Williams finally called 911, she casually said, "I think my daughter just killed herself. She's really rebellious." The family behaved as if nothing happened. During Williamses trial, other children reported that when you misbehave, you "go to the fires of hell." They were utterly and thoroughly brainwashed. After being removed from the house by child protective services, Hana's disabled brother, Immanuel, suffered from extreme PTSD. He had nightmares, he was profusely apologetic for his behaviors, he expected punishment, and he believed that he would be next to die.

Carri Williams, Hana's adoptive mother, was found guilty of homicide by abuse and sentenced to thirty-seven years of prison. Her husband, Larry, got twenty-eight years. Carri lost an appeal in which she was trying to prove that at the time of death, Hana was already sixteen and, therefore, legally could not be a victim of homicide by abuse. Documents and a testimony of a doctor from the Ethiopian orphanage proved that Hana was only thirteen. In 2015, the state appellate court upheld Ms. Williamson's conviction and reaffirmed that she was guilty of homicide by abuse of Hana and the first-degree assault of Immanuel. Since Ms. Williams strongly believed that she was only following Scripture, she did not show remorse and tried to have her conviction reversed based on technicalities. The courts did not see it that way.

Early years of the twenty-first century saw an abrupt surge of evangelical adoptions in the United States. A well-known incident took place in 2010 when following a devastating earthquake in Haiti, a bus chartered by the Baptist missionaries from Idaho was stopped while trying to cross the border into the Dominican Republic. The missionaries were accompanied by thirty-three Haitian children, supposedly orphaned by the disaster. Children had no required documents. It was soon discovered that they were not orphans. Most, if not all, had families and were kidnapped. The kids were returned to their families, and ten American missionaries were charged with kidnapping and child trafficking, although nine were later released.

Mega-families created by the fundamentalist Christians usually do not work. A family with that many children is no longer a family. It is a group home. Children cannot receive the individual attention that they need. Instead, they have chores that may be overwhelming, especially for the older ones who have to take care of their younger siblings.

Regardless, many fundamentalist Christians view adoption as a core of their religious beliefs and as a calling coming directly from God. Uneducated parents, often living in or close to poverty, built families of more than ten and sometimes more than twenty children. Many of the children adopted overseas were true orphans who lost their biological parents and who witnessed unimaginable carnage in their native lands. They were brought to America only to suffer years of malnutrition and abuse under the banner of Christianity. They have no ability and no means to reach out for help. They develop no practical skills and receive no formal education. After being kicked out by their adoptive parents, at the age of sixteen or eighteen, many end up on the streets with no jobs and no prospects for employment. To some, the United States became another Africa, only cold.

Printed in Great Britain
by Amazon

55547845R00101